PUBLIC RELATIONS IN BUSINESS, GOVERNMENT, AND SOCIETY

Reference Sources in the Social Sciences Series
Lubomyr R. Wynar, Series Editor

No. 1   *Sociology: A Guide to Reference and Information Sources.* By Stephen H. Aby.

No. 2   *Education: A Guide to Reference and Information Sources.* By Lois J. Buttlar.

No. 3   *Public Relations in Business, Government, and Society: A Bibliographic Guide.* By Anne B. Passarelli.

PUBLIC RELATIONS IN BUSINESS, GOVERNMENT, AND SOCIETY
A Bibliographic Guide

ANNE B. PASSARELLI
University of Washington
Seattle, Washington

1989

LIBRARIES UNLIMITED, INC.
Englewood, Colorado

LIBRARIES UNLIMITED, INC.
P.O. Box 3988
Englewood, Colorado 80155-3988

Library of Congress Cataloging-in-Publication Data

Passarelli, Anne B.
  Public relations in business, government, and society : a
bibliographic guide / Anne B. Passarelli.
    xiv, 129 p. 17x25 cm. -- (Reference sources in the social sciences series)
    Includes indexes.
    ISBN 0-87287-741-8
    1. Public relations--United States--Bibliography.   2. Public
relations--Bibliography.   I. Title.   II. Series.
Z7164.P957P37   1989
[HM263]
016.6592--dc20   89-12211
                                                                 CIP

Contents

Foreword ix

Introduction xi

1 — General and Historical Studies. 1
General and Theoretical Works. 1
Older Relevant Titles. 3
Textbooks 6
Historical and Biographical Works. 9
Historical Studies. 10
Personal Memoirs and Biographies. 11
Archives and Special Collections. 11

2 — Reference Resources on Public Relations Practice. 13
Reference Handbooks. 13
Practical Aspects and Techniques. 14
Directories. 20
Media Directories. 20
Directories of Public Relations Personnel. .23
Other Directories. 24
Organizations 25
Public Relations Practitioners. 25
Educational and Research Organizations. 29
Business and Interest-Group Organizations. 30
Other Organizations. 31
Education for Public Relations. 32
Career Guidance. 35

3 — Research Tools. 37
Periodicals. 37
Public Relations Journals. 37
Newsletters for Practitioners. 38
Scholarly Journals in Journalism and Communication. 40
Scholarly Journals in Business, Management, and
Marketing 41
Scholarly Journals in Political Science. 41
Other Scholarly Journals. 42
Journalism and Media Magazines. 43
Business and Marketing Magazines. 43
Magazines for Nonprofit Organization Managers. 45

3 — Research Tools — *Continued*

Bibliographies..45
Indexes..49
Online Resources...52
Publishers and Sponsors of Series........................55

4 — Corporate Public Relations.............................56
Image Building...56
       Corporate Identity...............................57
Economic Education.......................................58
Advocacy Advertising.....................................58
Issues Management..60
Consumer Relations.......................................62
Employee Relations.......................................63
Investor and Financial Relations.........................64
Public Affairs...66
Media Relations..68
Government Relations.....................................69
       Lobbying...71
       Political Action Committees......................72
Public Relations and Corporate Philanthropy..............73
Public Relations and Corporate Social Responsibility.....75
       The Corporate Social Audit.......................77
International Public Relations............................78
Applications in Particular Industries....................80
       Accounting.......................................80
       Entertainment Industry...........................80
       Financial Services...............................81
       Forest Industries................................81
       Public Utilities.................................81
       Services...81

5 — Public Relations in Government.........................82
Political Communication..................................82
Practical Works for Government Officials.................83
Public Information Offices in Action.....................84
Presidential Public Relations............................89

6 — Public Relations in American Politics..................92
Political Consultants and Campaigns......................92
Political Uses of New Technology.........................94
Other Aspects of the Politics-Media Relationship.........97

7—Public Relations in Nonprofit Organizations.........................98
  Nonprofit Organizations in General................................98
  Arts Organizations..100
  Charities...100
  Churches..100
  Educational Institutions..101
  Health-Care Organizations.......................................103
  Labor Organizations...104
  Libraries...105
  Museums...106
  Social-Welfare Organizations....................................106

  Author/Title Index..107
  Subject Index...125

Foreword

This series, Reference Sources in the Social Sciences, is intended to introduce librarians, researchers, and students to major sources within the social sciences disciplines. The series will cover the following disciplines: sociology, history, economics and business, political science, anthropology, education, psychology, and general social science reference sources.

The organization and content of each volume are shaped by bibliographic forms and subject structures of the individual disciplines. Since many subject areas within the social sciences are interrelated, some reference sections in the various volumes will have certain features in common (e.g., a section on general social science sources). Each volume in the series constitutes a unique reference tool, stressing the informational subject structure of the discipline, major reference publications, databases, and other relevant sources.

Public Relations in Business, Government, and Society will fill an important gap in the reference and business literature and provide useful tools for reference services and research in this area.

This volume is divided into seven chapters including general reference sources, reference sources on public relations functions in government, corporations and politics, and other relevant subjects.

Anne B. Passarelli is Head of the Business Administration Library at the University of Washington, Seattle, and previously she worked as a reference librarian at the same university. She is advisory board member of the forthcoming *Journal of Business & Finance Librarianship*.

L. R. Wynar
Series Editor

Introduction

THE SUBJECT OF PUBLIC RELATIONS

Whether we are aware of it or not, public relations pervades our daily lives. It is with us constantly in the media—in television talk shows, in newspaper feature columns and financial news, in magazine articles—and also in the activities of our community in the form of fund raisers, sponsored sports events, and appearances and speeches by public figures. Our mailboxes are filled with material promoting causes and political candidates, soliciting funds, and assessing public opinion. If the public relations function did not exist in the corporate sphere, we would notice the absence of more than mass mailings; we would also miss public television and charitable foundations, two institutions that depend heavily on corporate concern with image building. The entertainment industry would be quite different without the public relations work that promotes the images of athletes and film and musical stars. Our choice of popular reading would be much more limited without the public relations-generated articles about celebrities and consumer products that dominate the content of many magazines. In the political sphere, public relations techniques applied to campaign management have radically altered our political environment, especially with regard to the visibility of political candidates and the balance of power between individual candidate and political party.

What is public relations? First of all, public relations is a communication function, a conscious effort to influence other people and groups through communication processes. In this aspect, it has close ties to the marketing function. There is some disagreement in the literature on whether public relations is the superior function and marketing an aspect of it or vice versa. In either case, the approaches to planning, research, and program evaluation are quite similar whether the aim is to promote an organization's general image and goals or its products. In addition, public relations is viewed by some of its most lucid interpreters as a management function, a consciously managed expression of organizational identity that influences the planning process at all levels.

Three positive social effects of modern public relations are cited by Cutlip, Center, and Broom in *Effective Public Relations* (entry 48): organizations become more responsive to public opinion, the public interest is served through the airing of differing viewpoints on issues, and public understanding is improved by the information supplied to the media by public relations spokesmen.

Many definitions of public relations have been advanced over the years. From Edward L. Bernays, a public relations practitioner during most of this century and one of its most prolific writers, comes an often-quoted definition: "the attempt, by information, persuasion, and adjustment, to engineer public support for an activity, cause, movement, or institution." This definition, published in 1947 in an essay entitled The Engineering of Consent, characterizes Bernays' position as an advocate of the application of behavioral science research to public relations work; it also defines the process in terms of a one-way communication process, from the initiating source to the receiving public. More recently, definitions have tended to emphasize two-way communication, including feedback to the source affecting its subsequent actions, as an integral part of public relations. At the 1978 World Forum of Public Relations in Mexico City, the following definition was accepted: "the art and science of analyzing trends, predicting their consequences, counseling organization leaders, and implementing planned programs of action which will serve both the organization's and the public interest." A more general approach that retains the two-way emphasis is provided by Grunig and Hunt in their definition: "management of communication between an organization and its publics" (*Managing Public Relations*, 1984, p. 6; *see* entry 50). Another general definition, from public relations practitioner Art Stevens, is "the shaping of perception, through communication, for the achievement of positive goals" (*The Persuasion Explosion*, 1985, p. 18; *see* entry 19).

Just as there are different ways to define public relations, there also exist a number of terms for labeling essentially similar functions. In the corporate world, a 1986 survey by Jack O'Dwyer found corporate communications, public affairs, communications, and corporate relations to be popular alternative titles to public relations (*O'Dwyer's Directory of Corporate Communications*, 1986-87 ed., p. A5; *see* entry 168). Other descriptive terms often used include marketing communications, media relations, external relations, community relations, and issues management.

In addition to corporations, other uses of public relations are organizations and institutions of all types; public officials and agencies; the executive, legislative, and judicial branches of government; groups of citizens with common interests; and individuals, from political candidates to media stars. The publics at whom these efforts are aimed vary with the goals and public relationships of the source group. Corporate publics are probably the most diverse, including employees, employee families, customers, suppliers, dealers, industry groups and associations, stockholders and financial interest groups, the community, thought leaders, government, and the general public.

Along with the senders and receivers of public relations communications, a third group plays an important role in public relations—communication media, the instrument and channels through which messages are transmitted. These channels include newspapers, magazines, pamphlets, internal newsletters, annual and other corporate reports, radio and television, and educational literature as well as meetings, speeches, exhibits, tournaments, tours, and all sorts of special events.

This bibliography represents a wide range of views concerning the proper role of public relations. The variety of viewpoints reflects, in part, the confusion generated by the fact that the term *public relations* has three distinct referents: it is used to describe a general communication and management activity, a particular type of consulting entity (public relations counsel or agency), and also the specific techniques of communication. These techniques are centered on writing skills, since the tools of the public relations worker are the news release, broadcast script, newsletter, brochure, position paper, speech, and feature article. Some writers define public relations practice strictly in terms of this type of publicity work. Historically, these products of public relations work have been described in unflattering terms, often by representatives of the media (as puffery, for example, and its practitioners as flacks). In fact, the media and the public relations practitioner share a relationship of mutual dependence, although the American ideal of a free press makes reporters uneasy about this relationship.

A definition of modern public relations practice found in many of the current texts presents it as a four-step process in which the actual act of communicating is only one element in a larger framework. Other basic elements are (1) defining the situation or problem with the aid of social-science research techniques, (2) drawing up a strategic plan, and (3) evaluating the results of communication and using this feedback for modification of the first two steps in the process. Another commonly encountered four-step model for the practice of public relations is described by the acronym *RACE*, in which the letters represent the words *research, action, communicating*, and *evaluating*. Cutlip, Center, and Broom (entry 48) take a broader view, seeing the organization in a systems framework with the public relations function as the organization's adaptive subsystem working to maintain mutually beneficial relationships with the external environment. This model is particularly applicable in a corporate setting. However, the other major generators of public relations communications—government, political candidates and interest groups, and nonprofit organizations and institutions—function most effectively when they adopt the four-step approach.

Ironically, the practice of public relations has an image problem in our society. For one thing, it suffers from identity confusion, as suggested by the variety of titles applied to its activities and the lack of a single generally accepted definition. In addition, its persuasive aspects have been viewed as manipulative, akin to propaganda, and its stated goal of encouraging a variety of viewpoints in the public forum has been criticized as a rationalization for the monopolizing of public media by the holders of power. The fact that over the past two decades modern corporations have lost credibility with the American public, noted by many observers and documented by Lipset and Schneider (entry 13), indicates that their public relations functions have been less than effective. Public relations advocates view this situation as evidence of a continuing lack of commitment to public relations in the corporation. Their goal is to institutionalize the function and have it recognized as a distinct, executive-level area of responsibility, even a profession, requiring special skills and educational preparation. The Public Relations Society of America (PRSA), the major membership organization in the field, has developed a code of professional ethics, Standards for the Practice of Public Relations, as a step toward controlling the quality of the practice. There is also a movement, led by Bernays, to develop and apply licensing standards in the field; this is a controversial issue, however, with fear of external regulation on the one side and desire for professional recognition on the other.

SCOPE OF THIS BIBLIOGRAPHY

This compilation of writings and resources on the subject of public relations includes general descriptive works on contemporary and historical practice; some representative works on the theoretical bases from the fields of sociology, political science, communication, and marketing; and studies of the social and political effects of its applications. It is selective rather than comprehensive, with the intent of providing a starting point for further research on the various topics presented in this general survey. Annotated citations are included for monographs, bibliographies and indexes, reference works and directories, organizations, and periodical titles. To enumerate the specific contents of periodical publications is not within the scope of this volume. Readers seeking lists of articles on the subject or its subtopics may consult the bibliography published annually in *Public Relations Review* (entry 282) and other entries in the bibliographies section of this work. The emphasis throughout is on American practice and on works published in the United States, although an effort has been made to include some material representing public relations practice and concerns in other countries. Most of the material cited has been published since 1970; the choice of this starting date was made in recognition of the thorough coverage of the subject by Alice Norton in her bibliography, *Public Relations: Information Sources* (entry 277), published in that year.

The book is divided into seven chapters, beginning with general information sources; this is followed by two chapters devoted to reference resources, including handbooks, practical guides, directories, organizations, tools for educational and career information, periodicals, bibliographies, and indexes. Sources of information on public relations functions and effects in corporations, government, politics, and nonprofit organizations make up the final four chapters.

No bibliography can satisfy all users' needs, and each reflects the preferences and biases of its compiler. The topical arrangement of this volume may please some users who want to study particular aspects of public relations, while some others may object to the short annotations and omission of periodical articles. Multiple access points are provided through the topical and format divisions and through the author/title and subject indexes to meet the needs of users who seek an introduction on particular authors, titles, or topics.

Basic bibliographic information is provided for each title. Publishers' offices are listed according to their current or last reported location. Where the work cited includes footnotes or end-of-chapter references, the annotation *notes* appears; the inclusion of a bibliography is also noted. Short, descriptive annotations are included for most titles, based on examination of most of the cited items. The exceptions consist of a few titles that could not be located for examination but appeared to warrant inclusion as well as some of the media directories, and titles published or revised as the manuscript was being completed.

1

General and Historical Studies

GENERAL AND THEORETICAL WORKS

The titles in this section provide general overviews on the modern practice of public relations plus background information from various social science disciplines (communication, sociology, social psychology, marketing and political science) to clarify its theoretical foundations.

1. Altheide, David L., and Johnson, John M. **Bureaucratic Propaganda**. Newton, MA: Allyn & Bacon, 1980. 256 p. bibliography.
   A scholarly study, using communication and organization theory and based on an examination of official government reports, of the ways in which organizations promote themselves and create "reality" through their public records.

2. Awad, Joseph F. **The Power of Public Relations**. New York: Praeger, 1985. 158 p. notes.
   This book, written by a corporate public relations executive, presents a positive picture of public relations. In short chapters the author covers the major aspects of corporate practice. A chapter on public relations in the arts is included.

3. Bernays, Edward L. **The Later Years: Public Relations Insights, 1956-1986**. Rhinebeck, NY: Public Relations Quarterly, 1987. 152 p.
   A collection of writings over the past 30 years by one of the pioneers in the field in which he expresses his concerns about modern public relations practice. (Not examined.)

4. Black, Sam, ed. **Public Relations in the 1980s**. Proceedings of the Eighth Public Relations World Congress, London, May 1979. Oxford, England: Pergamon, 1980. 225 p.
   The participants consider specific problems in public relations practice as well as general concerns, such as educational preparation, problems of multinationals, and professional standards.

5. Blyskal, Jeff, and Blyskal, Marie. **PR: How the Public Relations Industry Writes the News**. New York: Morrow, 1985. 241 p. notes.
   The authors accuse journalists of putting freedom of the press at risk by allowing the public relations industry to shape the news. Areas of public relations activity that are considered include business and product publicity, the entertainment industry, crisis reporting, and politics.

6. Cantor, Bill. **Experts in Action: Inside Public Relations**. Edited by Chester Burger. Longman Series in Public Communication. White Plains, NY: Longman, 1984. 460 p.

Collected essays by public relations professionals on all aspects of their work. The appendix contains sample job descriptions and a glossary of terms. This book would be especially useful reading for persons entering the field. New edition published in 1988 (510 p.; not examined).

7. Cialdini, Robert B. **Influence: Science and Practice**. Glenview, IL: Scott, Foresman, 1985. 264 p. bibliography.

A text suitable for general readers, this study in social psychology examines six principles of compliance seeking. Relevant as background reading for an understanding of social influence. (Second edition, published in 1988, not examined.)

8. Fine, Seymour H. **The Marketing of Ideas and Social Issues**. New York: Praeger, 1981. 227 p. notes.

Public relations is limited to "the promotion of rapport, goodwill, or image" (p. xii) in this marketing-oriented study of the means by which socially beneficial information is disseminated, but this work presents a useful framework for understanding the public relations environment.

9. Henry, Kenneth. **Defenders and Shapers of the Corporate Image**. New Haven, CT: College & University Press, 1972. 240 p. notes.

Within a sociological framework, the author examines the professionalization process in public relations using data from a survey of practitioners. He finds that working in large corporations tends to inhibit the development of a separate professional identity.

10. Hill & Knowlton executives, eds. **Critical Issues in Public Relations**. Englewood Cliffs, NJ: Prentice-Hall, 1975. 234 p.

A collection consisting mostly of reprints of short speeches on a broad range of topics relating to public relations practice.

11. Jowett, Garth S., and O'Donnell, Victoria. **Propaganda and Persuasion**. Newbury Park, CA: Sage, 1986. 236 p. bibliography.

Persuasion (communication to influence) is distinguished from its subfield, propaganda (manipulation for a desired end), in this survey of communication research. Five case studies that show the techniques and uses of persuasive communication are presented. The authors' aim is to heighten awareness of propaganda so that we are not controlled by it. An extensive bibliography is included.

12. Lerbinger, Otto. **Designs for Persuasive Communication**. Englewood Cliffs, NJ: Prentice-Hall, 1972. 283 p. notes.

The author presents five persuasion models: stimulus-response, cognitive, motivational, social, and personality. Designs based on interpersonal and mass communication are discussed, and the literature of attitude formation is reviewed.

13. Lipset, Seymour M., and Schneider, William. **The Confidence Gap: Business, Labor, and Government in the Public Mind**. rev. ed. Baltimore, MD: Johns Hopkins University Press, 1987. 460 p. notes.

A summary of public opinion polls, first published in 1983. The authors find that public confidence in institutions is shaped, for the most part, by actual events.

14. **Opinion of the Publics**. motion picture. New York: Institute for Public Relations Research and Education, 1972. 16mm. 37 min., color.

A documentary film on the theory and practice of public relations. Available at no cost from Modern Talking Picture Service, 5000 Park Ave. North, St. Petersburg, FL 33709. The Institute for Public Relations Research and Education, producer of this film, expects to prepare a new, up-to-date videotape on the subject in 1989 (not examined).

15. Pavlik, John V. **Public Relations: What Research Tells Us**. Newbury Park, CA: Sage, 1987. 151 p. notes. bibliography.

A critical study of the research process with brief summaries of over three hundred research findings, a bibliographic essay, and an extensive bibliography. Intended as a supplementary text for undergraduate courses.

16. Rein, Irving J.; Kotler, Philip; and Stoller, Martin R. **High Visibility**. New York: Dodd, Mead, 1987. 366 p. notes.

A study of a single area of public relations practice, the celebrity industry. The authors apply marketing concepts in this context.

17. Schiller, Herbert I. **The Mind Managers**. Boston: Beacon, 1973. 214 p. notes.

The author views the military-industrial establishment as the source and controller of most public information. Therefore, this work is more on agenda setting than public relations, but its point of view is useful for understanding the modern public relations environment.

18. Steinberg, Charles S. **Creation of Consent: Public Relations in Practice**. New York: Hastings, 1975. 315 p. bibliography.

A thorough treatment of public relations work in corporations, nonprofit organizations, government, and international situations. The author includes twelve organizational public relations case studies.

19. Stevens, Art. **The Persuasion Explosion: Your Guide to the Power and Influence of Contemporary Public Relations**. Washington, DC: Acropolis, 1985. 224 p.

A readable work by a public relations practitioner that documents the importance of public relations in modern society.

OLDER RELEVANT TITLES

The following titles represent some of the most important older works in public relations and related disciplines. They are included for this reason, even though their pre-1970 publication dates put them outside the stated scope of this bibliography.

20. Bernays, Edward L. **Biography of an Idea: Memoirs of Public Relations Counsel Edward L. Bernays**. New York: Simon & Schuster, 1965. 849 p. notes.

A personal chronicle of public relations as seen and practiced by Bernays, whose career has spanned a large part of the twentieth century.

21. Bernays, Edward L., ed. **The Engineering of Consent**. Norman, OK: University of Oklahoma Press, 1955. 246 p.
   Articles by Bernays and others on public relations practice.

22. Boorstin, Daniel J. **The Image, or What Happened to the American Dream**. New York: Atheneum, 1961. 315 p. bibliographic essay.
   A study of the replacement of news with pseudo-events, heroes with celebrities, travelers with tourists, literature with condensations and film versions, ideal with images, and the American dream with illusions that are confused with reality. In a 1972 reissue the title was changed to *The Image: A Guide to Pseudo-Events in America*.

23. Cherington, Paul W., and Gillen, Ralph L. **The Business Representative in Washington: A Report on the Roundtable Discussions of 19 Washington Representatives on Their Job As They See It**. Washington, DC: Brookings, 1962. 134 p.
   A study of how corporate government relations activity is actually conducted, including a consideration of internal and external relationships and a discussion of future trends.

24. Cornwell, Elmo E., Jr. **Presidential Leadership of Public Opinion**. Bloomington, IN: Indiana University Press, 1965. 370 p. notes.
   A study of U.S. presidents from Theodore Roosevelt to John Kennedy examining the power of the presidential image, the growth of the White House public relations function, development of press conferences, and the media revolution during this period.

25. Golden, L. L. L. **Only by Public Consent: American Corporations Search for Favorable Opinion**. New York: Hawthorn Books, 1968. 386 p.
   The importance of assessing public opinion and gaining public approval is illustrated through four corporate case histories. Subsequent events add a note of irony to some of the examples used (General Motors and American Telephone & Telegraph in particular). A final chapter considers the ethics of public relations. The author was a longtime columnist for *The Saturday Review*.

26. Hiebert, Ray E. **Courtier to the Crowd: The Story of Ivy Lee and the Development of Public Relations**. Ames, IA: Iowa State University Press, 1966. 351 p. notes. bibliography.
   A study of one of the pioneers in public relations work in the first part of the twentieth century, based on the author's doctoral dissertation.

27. Hiebert, Ray E., ed. **The Press in Washington: Sixteen Top Newsmen Tell How the News Is Collected, Written and Communicated from the World's Most Important Capitol**. New York: Dodd, Mead, 1966. 233 p.
   A collection of essays, from the journalistic viewpoint, describing problems encountered in covering government news.

28. Kelley, Stanley, Jr. **Professional Public Relations and Political Power**. Baltimore, MD: Johns Hopkins University Press, 1956. 247 p. notes.
   Of historical interest as the first study of political consultants' activity, based on research between 1949 and 1952.

29. Lippmann, Walter. **Public Opinion**. New York: Macmillan, 1922. 427 p. notes.

In a key historical work, Lippmann applies contemporary psychological research in explaining the behavior of the American public.

30. MacNeil, Robert. **The People Machine: The Influence of Television on American Politics**. New York: Harper, 1968. 362 p. notes.

An early examination of the use of television in political campaigns.

31. McGinniss, Joe. **The Selling of the President, 1968**. New York: Trident Press, 1969. 253 p.

An insider's view of the Nixon campaign, revealing how style replaced substance in political campaigning.

32. Milbrath, Lester W. **The Washington Lobbyists**. Chicago: Rand McNally, 1963. 431 p. bibliography.

This is an old but classic study of lobbying, based on interviews.

33. Nimmo, Dan D. **Newsgathering in Washington: A Study in Political Communication**. New York: Atherton, 1964. 282 p. bibliography.

A study of the nature of the relationships between government public information officers and Washington reporters in which both groups are found to do an inadequate job of informing the public.

34. Perry, James M. **The New Politics: The Expanding Technology of Political Manipulation**. New York: C. N. Potter, 1968. 230 p. notes.

An early examination of campaign management written by a political journalist, including chapters on political-management firms, polling techniques, uses of electronic data processing, and television.

35. Pimlott, John A. R. **Public Relations and American Democracy**. Princeton, NJ: Princeton University Press, 1951. 265 p. notes.

An examination of government public relations functions, both political and administrative, noting the lack of a two-way communication model and comparing public relations with propaganda.

36. Pollard, James E. **The Presidents and the Press**. New York: Macmillan, 1947. 866 p.

This original volume examines U.S. presidents up to Harry Truman. A second volume, published in 1964, covers the period from Truman to Lyndon Johnson. The focus is on news conferences.

37. Raucher, Alan R. **Public Relations and Business, 1900-1929**. Johns Hopkins University Studies in Historical and Political Science, series 86, no. 2. Baltimore, MD: Johns Hopkins University Press, 1968. 178 p. bibliography.

A scholarly historical study in which public relations is seen as an aspect of corporate development as well as a vocation emerging from the growth of modern communications media.

38. Robinson, Edward J. **Public Relations and Survey Research: Achieving Organizational Goals in a Communication Context**. New York: Appleton-Century-Crofts, 1969. 282 p. notes.

Application of social- and behavioral-science research tools to public relations practice. This work was prepared with support from the Institute for Public Relations Research and Education.

39. Ross, Irwin. **The Image Merchants: The Fabulous World of Public Relations**. New York: Doubleday, 1959. 288 p.

A popular survey of public relations practice in the fifties.

40. Salinger, Pierre. **With Kennedy.** New York: Doubleday, 1966. 476 p.

The personal account of President Kennedy's press secretary. Another interesting source on the Kennedy administration's public relations is *Kennedy and the Press: The News Conferences* (edited by Harold W. Chase and Allen H. Lerman; New York: Crowell, 1965).

41. Simon, Morton J. **Public Relations Law**. New York: Appleton-Century-Crofts, 1969. 882 p. notes. bibliography.

A thorough and readable survey of legal issues that relate to public relations practice, written for both lawyers and practitioners. Topics include, among others, copyright, censorship, privacy and defamation, deceptive trade practices, industrial espionage, financial disclosure, lobbying and government regulation, and contests and sponsorship of events. Cases are cited throughout. In 1988, the Institute for Public Relations Research and Education published a much-needed, updated treatment of this topic: *Public Relations and the Law*, by Frank E. Walsh (New York: IPRRE, 129 p.; not examined).

42. Simon, Raymond, ed. **Perspectives in Public Relations**. Norman, OK: University of Oklahoma Press, 1966. 353 p. notes.

An anthology of articles, speeches, case studies, and other pieces that illustrate the history and process of public relations. Many key historical documents and persons are represented here.

43. Wyckoff, Gene. **The Image Candidates: American Politics in the Age of Television**. New York: Macmillan, 1968. 274 p. notes.

A study of the political uses of television by a writer on Nixon's campaign team.

TEXTBOOKS

Textbooks for college and university instruction are useful in providing an overview of contemporary public relations practice and its place in our society. Current textbooks usually feature short, up-to-date bibliographies at the end of each chapter as suggestions for further reading. The texts listed here are primarily intended for communication and journalism courses, but there are a few examples from the business curriculum and one describing the emerging field of study of political communication. Note that textbooks are revised frequently; therefore, new editions of some of the following titles will probably be available by the time this list is published.

44.   Aram, John D. **Managing Business and Public Policy: Concepts, Issues and Cases**. Boston: Pitman, 1983. 583 p.

A text for business students explaining the business-public policy interface from a management viewpoint; includes readings and case studies.

45.   Aronoff, Craig E., and Baskin, Otis W. **Public Relations: The Profession and the Practice**. 2d ed. St. Paul, MN: West, 1988. 483 p.

A communication text arranged in sections on the profession, the process, publics, nonprofit and business practice, and critical issues. Short case studies are also included.

46.   Center, Allen H., and Walsh, Frank E. **Public Relations Practices: Managerial Case Studies and Problems**. 3d ed. Englewood Cliffs, NJ: Prentice-Hall, 1985. 470 p.

A book of case studies intended as supplementary reading for students.

47.   Crable, Richard E., and Vibbert, Steven L. **Public Relations As Communication Management**. Edina, MN: Bellwether Press, 1986. 436 p. notes.

An introductory text focusing on the communication and management aspects of public relations, with research, analysis, affecting, and reevaluating as basic functions.

48.   Cutlip, Scott M.; Center, Allen H.; and Broom, Glen M. **Effective Public Relations**. 6th ed. Englewood Cliffs, NJ: Prentice-Hall, 1985. 670 p. notes. bibliographies.

The most comprehensive text on the subject, a classic for many years. The contents have been updated regularly to maintain currency. The authors provide particularly useful end-of-chapter reading lists.

49.   Dunn, S. Watson. **Public Relations: A Contemporary Approach**. Homewood, IL: Irwin, 1986. 683 p.

The content of this text is organized into sections on background; techniques; and special problems, such as corporate communication, public relations in government and in associations of various kinds, international practices, and technological developments.

50.   Grunig, James E., and Hunt, Todd. **Managing Public Relations**. New York: Holt, Rinehart & Winston, 1984. 550 p. bibliographies.

A comprehensive text in which the authors examine the subject in a systems-theory conceptual framework and stress the importance of the two-way symmetric communication model. The general areas covered are the development of public relations, management aspects, programs, and communication techniques. Each chapter concludes with a list of additional readings.

51.   Hunt, Gary T. **Communication Skills in the Organization**. Englewood Cliffs, NJ: Prentice-Hall, 1980. 345 p.

A text for the study of organizational communication.

52.   Jefkins, Frank. **Public Relations**. Plymouth, England: MacDonald & Evans, 1980. 222 p.

A self-study text for the British public relations certification program, this work provides an overview of the subject from a British perspective.

53. Lovell, Ronald P. **Inside Public Relations**. Boston: Allyn & Bacon, 1982. 415 p.
A text designed for use by both journalism and business students.

54. Marston, John E. **Modern Public Relations**. New York: McGraw-Hill, 1979. 496 p.
An update of a 1963 work entitled *The Nature of Public Relations*. (Not examined.)

55. Moore, H. Frazier, and Kalupa, Frank. **Public Relations: Principles, Cases and Problems**. 9th ed. Homewood, IL: Irwin, 1985.
The latest edition has been enhanced with the addition of sections on issues management and international public relations. (Not examined.)

56. Newsom, Doug, and Carrell, Bob. **Public Relations Writing: Form and Style**. 2d ed. Wadsworth Series in Mass Communication. Belmont, CA: Wadsworth, 1986. 442 p. notes.
A comprehensive text on a limited subject; includes a summary of research findings to date on persuasion and attitude change. *Writing in Public Relations Practice* was the title of the first edition.

57. Newsom, Doug, and Scott, Alan. **This Is PR: The Realities of Public Relations**. 3d ed. Belmont, CA: Wadsworth, 1985. 518 p. notes.
A practical and readable introduction with annotated references and case studies. The authors have expanded the consideration of ethics and social responsibility and improved the general format from earlier editions. The appendix contains career guidance and the Public Relations Society of America code of professional standards.

58. Nimmo, Dan D. **Political Communication and Public Opinion in America**. Santa Monica, CA: Goodyear, 1978. 465 p. bibliographies.
Describing his work as an attempt to provide a comprehensive text in a new field, the author analyzes the elements and effects of political communication as practiced by "professional communicators." A valuable aspect of this work is its review of research studies on the subject.

59. Nolte, Lawrence W. **Fundamentals of Public Relations: Professional Guidelines, Concepts and Integrations**. 2d ed. New York: Pergamon, 1979. 516 p.
Sections deal with the nature of public relations, public opinion and publics, elements of a public relations program, and tools of the practice.

60. Norris, James S. **Public Relations**. Englewood Cliffs, NJ: Prentice-Hall, 1984. 286 p.
A text with short chapters, an easy-to-read format, and a practical orientation, apparently intended for undergraduate business students.

61. Reilly, Robert T. **Public Relations in Action**. 2d ed. Englewood Cliffs, NJ: Prentice-Hall, 1987. 480 p.
A basic, practical introduction to public relations activities and applications.

62. Schramm, Wilbur, and Porter, William E. **Men, Women, Messages, and Media: Understanding Human Communication**. 2d ed. New York: Harper, 1982. 278 p. notes. bibliographies.
A thorough and readable introduction to communication processes, theory, research, and the role of the mass media in modern society. The sections that are most relevant to public relations discuss effects of communication, television and the political process, media events, and advertising on television.

63. Seitel, Fraser P. **The Practice of Public Relations**. 3d ed. Columbus, OH: Charles E. Merrill, 1987. 616 p.

A comprehensive text by a public relations executive. Includes interviews with public relations practitioners and short case studies.

64. Simon, Raymond. **Public Relations: Concepts and Practices**. 3d ed. New York: Wiley, 1984. 442 p.

The author describes the public relations function, the process, and major contemporary concerns (legal, political, technological, ethical, and educational).

65. Simon, Raymond. **Public Relations Management: A Casebook**. 3d ed. Columbus, OH: Publishing Horizons, 1986. 280 p.

This book consists mainly of case studies, with some reprinted excerpts from writings of public relations leaders included to stimulate discussion. The case studies cover nonprofit organizational settings, business, and public relations counsel operations. It is intended for use in upper-level undergraduate classes, graduate courses, and continuing professional education.

66. Simons, Herbert W. **Persuasion: Understanding, Practice and Analysis**. Reading, MA: Addison-Wesley, 1976. 382 p. bibliography.

An overview of the topic with recommended readings and a useful bibliography.

67. Walsh, Frank E. **Public Relations Writer in a Computer Age**. Englewood Cliffs, NJ: Prentice-Hall, 1986. 274 p.

This text includes publicity-writing techniques and case studies. The title is rather misleading since the use of the computer in text preparation is not included.

68. Wilcox, Dennis L.; Ault, Philip H.; and Agee, Warren K. **Public Relations Strategies and Tactics**. New York: Harper, 1986. 645 p.

Organized into sections on role, process, strategy, applications, and techniques; includes a chapter on ethics in public relations practice and a useful list of references on public relations for special types of organizations. New edition in 1988, not examined.

HISTORICAL AND BIOGRAPHICAL WORKS

The major historical study specifically on public relations to appear since 1970 is Tedlow's work (entry 76). The Lasswell three-volume series (entry 72) is an important historical survey on the subject of communication and propaganda that has considerable relevance for modern public relations. Also listed here are studies of U.S. presidents' use of public relations, early efforts at corporate image building, and an examination of Hitler's use of propaganda techniques. Some examples of personal memoirs are also included.

Historical Studies

69. Bogart, Leo. **Premises for Propaganda: The United States Information Agency's Operating Assumptions in the Cold War**. New York: Free Press, 1976. 250 p. bibliography.

A study of the information-generating activities of a government agency during the 1950s; includes techniques used by the agency's public information officers.

70. Galambos, Louis. **The Public Image of Big Business in America, 1880-1940: A Quantitative Study in Social Change**. Baltimore, MD: Johns Hopkins University Press, 1975. 324 p. notes.

The author uses content analysis of selected journals to reveal contemporary public attitudes toward the rise of giant corporations.

71. Herzstein, Robert E. **The War That Hitler Won: The Most Infamous Propaganda Campaign in History**. New York: Putnam, 1978. 491 p. notes.

A scholarly study of the state propaganda institutions in Germany under Hitler and their manipulation of the media.

72. Lasswell, Harold; Lerner, Daniel; and Speier, Hans, eds. **Propaganda and Communication in World History**. 3 vols. Honolulu, HA: East-West Center of the University of Hawaii, 1979-1980.

A comprehensive and scholarly survey on the political uses of communication, starting in ancient times and concluding with an examination of the contemporary situation and speculation about the future.

73. McQuaid, Kim. **Big Business and Presidential Power from FDR to Reagan**. New York: Morrow, 1982. 383 p. bibliography.

A historian's study on the development of the corporate-government relationship since the 1930s.

74. Olasky, Marvin N. **Corporate Public Relations: A New Historical Perspective**. Hillsdale, NJ: Lawrence Erlbaum, 1987. 180 p. bibliography.

This examination of industry's early efforts to inhibit competition, based on a study of the railroads, public utilities, and the publicist Ivy Lee, is an expansion of the author's earlier essay, "The Development of Corporate Public Relations, 1850-1930," *Journalism Monographs* no. 102 (April 1987). He advocates expansion of an area described as "private business relations," that is, business matters exempt from public disclosure.

75. Steele, Richard W. **Propaganda in an Open Society: The Roosevelt Administration and the Media, 1933-1941**. Westport, CT: Greenwood, 1985. 231 p. bibliography.

A historical examination of Roosevelt's management of government communication.

76. Tedlow, Richard S. **Keeping the Corporate Image: Public Relations and Business, 1900-1950**. Greenwich, CT: Jai Press, 1979. 233 p. notes. bibliography.

A valuable historical study, based on the author's doctoral dissertation, on the development of corporate public relations during its period of greatest growth.

Personal Memoirs and Biographies

77.   Barmash, Isadore. **Always Live Better Than Your Clients: The Fabulous Life and Times of Benjamin Sonnenberg**. New York: Dodd, Mead, 1983. 224 p.
   A biography of a prominent practitioner whose clients included Texaco, Lever Brothers, MGM, and Philip Morris.

78.   Kelley, F. Beverly. **It Was Better Than Work**. Gerald, MO: Patrice Press, 1982. 273 p.
   A publicist for the circus describes his career.

79.   Lipsen, Charles B., with Lesher, Stephan. **Vested Interest**. New York: Doubleday, 1977. 184 p.
   An anecdotal narrative by a union lobbyist.

80.   Powell, Jody. **The Other Side of the Story**. New York: Morrow, 1984. 322 p.
   Memoir of the White House press secretary under President Carter.

81.   Rogers, Henry C. **Walking the Tightrope: The Private Confessions of a Public Relations Man**. New York: Morrow, 1980. 256 p.
   One of the several books by this career public relations consultant. See also *Rogers' Rules for Success* (entry 134).

82.   Schorr, Daniel. **Clearing the Air**. Boston: Houghton Mifflin, 1977. 333 p. notes.
   A one-sided view of television news coverage during the Watergate period, important for its subject: the political pressures felt by network executives.

83.   Wood, Robert J., with Gunther, Max. **Confessions of a PR Man**. Bergenfield, NJ: New American Library, 1988. 269 p.
   An anecdotal memoir from a well-known public relations executive, the ex-chairman of Carl Byoir and Associates. Excerpts from this work appear in the July-August 1988 issue of *Public Relations Journal*.

ARCHIVES AND SPECIAL COLLECTIONS

The papers of several important figures in public relations history have been preserved and are available to scholars in the following institutions:

Mass Communications History Center, State Historical Society of Wisconsin. Madison, WI.
   Papers of Edward L. Bernays, John W. Hill, and Arthur W. Page.

Seely G. Mudd Manuscript Library, Princeton University. Princeton, NJ.
   Papers of Ivy L. Lee.

In addition, the archives of the National Association of Manufacturers, one of the early industry organizations practicing public relations, have been maintained. They are available at

Eleutherian Mills Historical Library. Wilmington, DE.

Other valuable collections relating to public relations are listed below (arranged by state).

CASE Reference Center, Council for Advancement and Support of Education. Washington, DC.

Journalism and Mass Communications Library, University of Illinois. Urbana, IL.

United States Army Information Center. Fort Benjamin. Harrison, IN.

Edward L. Bernays Public Relations Library. Cambridge, MA.

Public Affairs Information Services, General Motors Corporation. Detroit, MI.

Journalism Library, University of Missouri. Columbia, MO.

Burson-Marsteller Information Services. Chicago and New York.

Information Center, Public Relations Society of America. New York.

Milton Caniff Library, Ohio State University. Columbus, OH.

Nieman-Grant Reading Room, University of Wisconsin. Madison, WI.
    Includes the Frank Thayer Collection on the Law of Mass Communications.

2

Reference Resources on
Public Relations Practice

This chapter and the one that follows describe a variety of resources that may be consulted for more information on specific questions relating to public relations and its practice. Included in this chapter are reference handbooks and books on practical techniques, a sampling of directories used in practice, organizations for practitioners, information on educational preparation, and guides to public relations as a career.

REFERENCE HANDBOOKS

These encyclopedic guides are intended to serve as comprehensive resources on the subject. The Dilenschneider and Lesly volumes (entries 85 and 87, respectively) are standard works in the field and have been through numerous editions. A more specialized reference work on organizational communication is also included, as are two guides to communication terminology.

84.   Blake, Reed H., and Haroldsen, Edwin O. **A Taxonomy of Concepts in Communication**. New York: Hastings, 1975. 158 p. bibliography.
Sixty concepts relevant to communication are defined and described. (Each description is one to three pages long.) Public relations is one of these topics. The concepts are grouped in seven broad areas, including basic elements, forms of communication, types of material communicated, the process and its effects, mass media functions, the environment of communication, and investigative approaches.

85.   Dilenschneider, Robert L., and Forrestal, Dan J. **Public Relations Handbook**. 3d ed. Chicago: Dartnell, 1987. 916 p. bibliography.
The latest edition of a classic handbook, containing explanations of public relations functions and programs; separate sections on health-care public relations, nonprofit-organization public relations, and public affairs; award-winning cases; and, in an appendix, six lectures from an annual series sponsored by the Institute for Public Relations Research and Education.

86.   Jablin, Fredrick M., et al., eds. **Handbook of Organizational Communication: An Interdisciplinary Perspective**. Newbury Park, CA: Sage, 1987. 781 p. bibliographies.
The editors of this work represent the disciplines of speech communication, communication, business administration, and management. This research summary addresses theoretical issues and questions of context, structure, and process. The most relevant section for public relations is a chapter by George Cheney and Steven L. Vibbert on corporate discourse.

87. Lesly, Philip, ed. **Lesly's Public Relations Handbook**. 3d ed. Englewood Cliffs, NJ: Prentice-Hall, 1983. 718 p. bibliography.

An encyclopedic resource with fifty-four chapters contributed by experts in the field. The first two sections define public relations and describe its publics. Other sections explain its practice in various business settings, in politics and government, and in nonprofit institutions; give guidance on research; and provide detail on tools and techniques.

88. **Longman Dictionary of Mass Media and Communication**. Longman Series in Public Communication. White Plains, NY: Longman, 1982. 255 p.

A reference work covering all communication specializations, such as advertising, graphic and print media, theater, and data processing. Includes many technical terms but not basic concepts (e.g., propaganda) or proper names.

PRACTICAL ASPECTS AND TECHNIQUES

This section consists of practical guides to the technical aspects of public relations work. As it is by no means a complete guide to the material published since 1970, readers may wish to consult bibliographies and suggested readings contained in some of the listed works for more resources on particular techniques. Useful reading lists also can be found in the appropriate sections of many of the introductory public relations textbooks listed in the previous chapter.

89. Anson, Edward M. **How to Prepare and Write Your Employee Handbook**. New York: American Management Association Publications, 1984. 221 p.

A work in loose-leaf format consisting of a sample handbook with explanations accompanying each section.

90. Ashley, Paul P., with Hall, Camden M. **Say It Safely: Legal Limits in Publishing, Radio and Television**. Seattle, WA: University of Washington Press, 1976. 238 p.

A guide for journalists and advertising workers on an important aspect of communication.

91. Benn, Alec. **The 23 Most Common Mistakes in Public Relations**. New York: Amacom, 1982. 257 p.

Rules for effective communication illustrated with case histories.

92. Bernays, Edward L. **Public Relations**. Norman, OK: University of Oklahoma Press, 1952. 374 p. bibliography.

One of Bernays' early practical guides, reprinted in 1980.

93. Bernstein, Alan B. **Emergency Public Relations Manual**. New Brunswick, NJ: PASE, Inc., 1981. 94 p. notes.

Public relations for disaster-response situations, including forms, checklists, and work sheets in a loose-leaf format.

94. Bivens, Thomas. **Handbook for Public Relations Writing**. Lincolnwood, IL: National Textbook, 1987. 312 p.

Given a generally favorable review in *Public Relations Review* (Winter 1987). (Not examined.)

95. Black, Sam, and Sharpe, Melvin L. **Practical Public Relations: Common-Sense Guidelines for Business and Professional People**. Englewood Cliffs, NJ: Prentice-Hall, 1983. 214 p.

This work by two well-known practitioners is directed at nonspecialists and includes an examination of the international aspects of public relations practice.

96. Bloomenthal, Howard. **Promoting Your Cause**. New York: Funk & Wagnalls, 1971. 248 p. bibliography.

Basic advice on communicating ideas, written in a direct and expository style.

97. Brody, E. W. **The Business of Public Relations**. New York: Praeger, 1987. 327 p. bibliography.

This work focuses on the management of a public relations consultancy. The author uses a systems framework in which the organization comprises psychological, social, political, and technological internal subsystems. All managerial functions are covered, and model programs are presented as examples.

98. Brody, E. W. **Public Relations Programming and Production**. New York: Praeger, 1988. 319 p. bibliographies.

A study of the preparation and delivery of public relations communications and the channels used to disseminate these messages.

99. Chambers, Wicke, and Asher, Spring. **TV PR: How to Promote Yourself, Your Product, Your Service or Your Organization on Television**. Atlanta, GA: Chase Communications, 1986. 126 p.

A practical guide to getting television-show bookings and presenting guests. Written in a popular style with illustrations and examples. Topics include use of public relations agencies; preparation of media kits, visuals and demos; developing contacts; presenting a proposal; planning a guest appearance; and what producers look for.

100. Cole, George. **The News Connection: Effective Public Relations**. video recording. Spokane, WA: Media West, 1979. Beta, VHS, or ¾ in. 39 min., color.

Reviewed by Hiebert in *Public Relations Review* (Summer 1980). (Not examined.) Updated version to be produced in 1989.

101. Corrado, Frank M. **Media for Managers: Communications Strategy for the Eighties**. Englewood Cliffs, NJ: Prentice-Hall, 1984. 225 p. notes.

The author describes areas of internal and external communication management, mainly in the corporate environment; explains how it is practiced; and suggests future trends. Issues applicable to government and nonprofit sector communications are treated in an appendix.

102. Coulson-Thomas, Colin. **Public Relations Is Your Business: A Guide for Every Manager**. London: Business Books, 1981. 273 p.

A British overview of corporate public relations for senior managers and directors. The major areas of public relations practice are described and short cases are provided.

103. Culligan, Matthew J., and Greene, Dolph. **Getting Back to the Basics of Public Relations and Publicity**. New York: Crown, 1982. 111 p. bibliography.

Practical advice on public communication functions in a corporate setting with lists of ideas, tips, and a few case histories.

104. Daubert, Harold E. **Industrial Publicity**. New York: Wiley, 1974. 225 p.

Limited to the message-development and delivery functions.

105. Dessart, George. **More Than You Want to Know About Public Service Announcements**. Denver, CO: National Broadcast Association for Community Affairs, 1982. 34 p.

Subtitled *A Guide to Production and Placement of Effective Public Service Announcements on Radio and Television*. A brief, practical introduction, written by a public affairs television executive, which also explains community-interest programming regulations.

106. Detz, Joan. **How to Write and Give a Speech**. New York: St. Martin, 1984. 143 p.

Using short chapters and a prescriptive style, the author (a corporate speechwriter) gives practical guidance on speech preparation and delivery. A listing of useful resources (sources for quotations, statistics, and facts) is included.

107. Douglas, George A. **Writing for Public Relations**. Columbus, OH: Charles E. Merrill, 1980. 183 p.

This work covers a variety of writing assignments with examples; limited to stylistic considerations.

108. Druck, Kalman B.; Fiur, Merton; and Bates, Don, eds. **New Technology and Public Relations: A Guide for Public Relations and Public Affairs Practitioners**. New York: Institute for Public Relations Research and Education, 1986. 170 p.

Twenty-five contributors examine the broad areas of computers, satellite transmission, cable television, and telephone services, showing through case studies and practical advice how these technologies can improve speed, efficiency, and quantity of information access. New edition available in 1989.

109. Ehrenkranz, Lois B., and Kahn, Gilbert R., eds. **Public Relations/Publicity: A Key Link in Communications**. New York: Fairchild, 1983. 231 p. bibliography.

Narrowly focused on publicity activities, this work is designed for beginning practitioners and as an introductory text. A glossary of terms is included.

110. Goldman, Jordan. **Public Relations in the Marketing Mix: Introducing Vulnerability Relations**. Chicago: Crain, 1984. 165 p.

Practical advice on proactive public relations, but limited to a marketing framework.

111.   Halpern, Burton M. **Tell It to the World: A Guide to International Public Relations**. Jerusalem: Gefen Books, 1982. 150 p.

An international treatment limited to publicity and image building and lacking any discussion of cultural influences in public relations.

112.   Hendrix, Jerry A. **Public Relations Cases**. Belmont, CA: Wadsworth, 1988. 447 p.

This work, for the most part, consists of winning cases from the annual Silver Anvil competition sponsored by the Public Relations Society of America. Reviewed in *Public Relations Review* (Summer 1988). (Not examined.)

113.   Hiebert, Ray E., ed. **Precision Public Relations**. White Plains, NY: Longman, 1988. 396 p. bibliography.

A reader in public relations with many articles selected from past issues of *Public Relations Review*. Reviewed in *Public Relations Review* (Summer 1988). (Not examined.)

114.   Howard, Carole, and Mathews, Wilma. **On Deadline: Managing Media Relations**. Longman Series in Public Communication. White Plains, NY: Longman, 1985. 205 p. bibliography.

A practical description of this aspect of public relations practice for corporate media-relations personnel.

115.   Howard, Wilfred, ed. **The Practice of Public Relations**. London: Heinemann, 1982. 250 p.

Prepared for the Communication, Advertising and Marketing Education Foundation and the Institute of Marketing as an introductory text for British students; contains essays by British practitioners.

116.   Hudson, Howard P. **Publishing Newsletters**. New York: Scribner, 1982. 205 p. bibliography.

A book of practical advice from a newsletter publisher on the preparation of corporate, union, and association publications.

117.   Klein, Ted, and Danzig, Fred. **Publicity: How to Make the Media Work for You**. 2d ed. New York: Scribner, 1985. 262 p.

The authors explain how to exploit the media (their phrase) for public relations purposes.

118.   Klein, Walter J. **The Sponsored Film**. New York: Hastings, 1976. 210 p.

An introductory guide to the development of the sponsored film industry and the uses, production, and marketing of such films.

119.   Klepper, Michael M. **Getting Your Message Out: How to Get, Use and Survive Radio and Television Air Time**. Englewood Cliffs, NJ: Prentice-Hall, 1984. 174 p. notes.

A manual for business or institutional managers without expertise in public relations techniques.

120.   Lewis, H. Gordon. **How to Handle Your Own PR**. Chicago: Nelson-Hall, 1976. 251 p.

A practical guide, mainly to publicity activities, including suggestions for specific types of businesses. The author states that anyone with self-confidence can do public relations but that contacts and preparation are helpful.

121.   Londgren, Richard E. **Communication by Objectives: A Guide to Productive and Cost-Effective Public Relations and Marketing**. Englewood Cliffs, NJ: Prentice-Hall, 1983. 200 p. notes.

The author stresses the importance of planned communication, verbal and nonverbal, and gives guidelines for logical problem analysis.

122.   Martin, Dick. **The Executive's Guide to Handling a Press Interview**. rev. ed. Babylon, NY: Pilot Books, 1985. 47 p.

Contains practical techniques and a checklist. Topics include interviews, press conferences, and media appearances. Related titles available from this publisher include *How to Handle Speechwriting Assignments* and *Preparing Effective Presentations*.

123.   McCrummen, J. B. **A Guide to Community Advocacy Skills**. Olympia, WA: Strategies for Democracy Fund, 1981. 128 p. bibliography.

Written by a public-interest-group public relations consultant who explains how to organize, raise funds, work with the media, and influence the legislative process.

124.   The Media Institute. **Using New Communications Technologies: A Guide for Organizations**. Washington, DC: The Media Institute, 1986. 57 p.

This short, introductory guide is intended to assist nonprofit organizations and small corporations in improving their communication techniques. Topics covered include computer use, satellite technology, cable TV, and videotape.

125.   Nager, Norman R., and Harrell, T. Allen. **Public Relations Management by Objectives**. Longman Series in Public Communication. White Plains, NY: Longman, 1984. 404 p. notes.

A practical guide to implementing management by objectives in public relations work; also provides the theoretical and research framework. Short case studies are included and two models for public relations management are described.

126.   Nager, Norman R., and Truitt, Richard H. **Strategic Public Relations Counseling: Models from the Counselors Academy**. White Plains, NY: Longman, 1987. 376 p.

An introduction to the work of the public relations counseling firm. The contents are based on interviews and include public relations activities and tools and aspects of the counselor-client relationship.

127.   Nolte, Lawrence W., and Wilcox, Dennis L. **Effective Publicity: How to Reach a Public**. New York: Wiley, 1984. 367 p.

In this comprehensive treatment of the work of publicists, publicity is viewed as a form of communication that supports the public relations and marketing functions.

128.   Nowlan, Stephen E., and Shayon, Diana R. **Leveraging the Impact of Public Affairs: A Guidebook Based on Practical Experience for Corporate Public Affairs Executives**. Philadelphia, PA: Human Resources Network, 1984. 385 p.

Prepared by a corporate consulting firm, this volume focuses on planning and communication strategies for effective action in the areas of government and community relations, internal communications, corporate giving programs, and relations with public interest groups. Includes exercises and checklists; no index.

129. Parkhurst, William. **How to Get Publicity (and Make the Most of It When You've Got It)**. New York: Times Books, 1985. 245 p. bibliography.
     Written in an informal style with examples and practical advice.

130. Pickens, Judy E., et al., eds. **Without Bias: A Guidebook for Nondiscriminatory Communication**. 2d ed. New York: Wiley (for the International Association of Business Communicators), 1982. 200 p. bibliography.
     Short sections examine different kinds of discrimination (racial, sexual, handicapped) and situations in which bias may occur (visuals, meetings). Positive and negative examples are included. (1977 edition examined.)

131. Public Management Institute. **Successful Public Relations Techniques**. San Francisco, CA: Public Management Institute, 1980. 449 p. bibliography.
     A loose-leaf manual prepared by a commercial publisher of materials for the improvement of nonprofit management. It covers planning and getting organized for a public relations program as well as basic tools for communicating with the media and preparing publications. Numerous checklists, work sheets, exercises, and examples are included.

132. Ridgway, Judith. **Successful Media Relations: A Practitioner's Guide**. Aldershot, England: Gower, 1984. 214 p.
     Public relations is limited to press relations in this British volume, a practical but not detailed treatment of the topic. British media and information sources are included.

133. Risley, Curtis, ed. **Ayer Public Relations and Publicity Style Book**. 7th ed. Fort Washington, PA: IMS Press, 1983. unnumbered pages.
     A guide to copywriting in the Associated Press style. The tabbed chapters deal with types of forms, headlines, construction, punctuation, spelling, capitalization, abbreviations, and numbers.

134. Rogers, Henry C. **Rogers' Rules for Success**. New York: St. Martin, 1984. 285 p.
     Case histories written in a popular style by the founder of a Hollywood public relations firm.

135. Sahai, Baldeo. **Public Relations: A Scientific Approach**. New Delhi: Standing Conference of Public Enterprises, 1980. 336 p.
     A general introduction to the practice of public relations in India.

136. Selame, Elinor, and Selame, Joe. **Developing a Corporate Identity: How to Stand Out in the Crowd**. New York: Chain Store Publishing, 1975. 246 p. notes.
     The visual symbol is presented as the major element in a corporate identity. This work explains how to develop this identity through symbol selection, architecture, signage, and package design.

137. Selnow, Gary W., and Crano, William D., eds. **Planning, Implementing and Evaluating Targeted Communication Programs: A Manual for Business Communicators**. Westport, CT: Quorum, 1987. 291 p. bibliography.
     The editors' backgrounds are communication and psychology. In addition to their contributions, this work includes six essays by other media specialists and a literature review. Reviewed in *Public Relations Review* (Winter 1987). (Not examined.)

138. Soderberg, Norman R. **Public Relations for the Entrepreneur and the Growing Business**. Chicago: Probus, 1986. 243 p. bibliography.

In this book, written from a marketing publicity viewpoint for the small businessman, the author prescribes appropriate activities and tactics.

139. Sperber, Nathaniel N., and Lerbinger, Otto. **The Manager's Public Relations Handbook**. Reading, MA: Addison-Wesley, 1982. 334 p.

This book consists of fifty-six topic-specific checklists for managers, each with a short introduction. The format is succinct and practical. Topics covered include crises; media relations; consumer affairs; employee, community, and financial relations; special events; and public relations management activities.

140. Tarver, Jerry. **The Corporate Speech Writer's Handbook: A Guide for Professionals in Business, Agencies and the Public Sector**. Westport, CT: Quorum, 1987. 185 p. bibliography.

The author, a practitioner and scholar in speech communication, includes principles and practical techniques and an overview of the work of speech-writers.

141. Weiner, Richard. **Professional's Guide to Publicity**. New York: Richard Weiner, Inc., 1975. 133 p.

A manual for press publicity covering format, style, and distribution and including annotated samples. Third revised edition published New York: Public Relations, 1982. 176 p. (Not examined.)

142. White, Jan V. **Using Charts and Graphs: 1000 Ideas for Visual Persuasion**. New York: Bowker, 1984. 202 p.

Ten types of visual charts and graphs and their applications are described in this specialized work; the final chapter is on technical production skills.

143. Yale, David R. **The Publicity Handbook**. New York: Bantam, 1982. 300 p.

A comprehensive, practical guide on the subject of publicity, including a list of directories and other materials of interest to working publicists.

DIRECTORIES

The tools used in public relations work include a variety of national and local media directories. No attempt has been made in this book to include local or regional media directories (except for the Washington, DC, news scene), but the most widely used titles with national or international coverage are listed here.

Media Directories

144. **All TV Publicity Outlets Nationwide**. New Milford, CT: Public Relations Plus. (Annual)

A listing of cable and regular television programs using guests, films, or prepared scripts. (*See* entry 151.)

145. **Bacon's International Publicity Checker.** Chicago: Bacon's. (Annual)
Information and market classifications for trade and business publications and newspapers in Western Europe.

146. **Bacon's Media Alerts: Directory of Media Calendars and Editorial Profiles.** Chicago: Bacon's. (Annual with bimonthly updates.)
Includes, for each magazine and newspaper listed, circulation, lead times, editorial profile, and information about special issues or editorial focus.

147. **Bacon's Publicity Checker.** Chicago: Bacon's. (Annual with quarterly updates.)
Brief summary information on magazines (grouped into market classifications) and newspapers in the United States. Seventeen thousand publications are included in the 1987 edition.

148. **Bacon's Radio/TV Directory.** Chicago: Bacon's. (Annual with quarterly updates.)
Includes television and radio stations by state, networks, major market maps, and call-letter indexes. For each station gives address and key personnel, programming information, and target-audience profile.

149. **Broadcasting/Cablecasting Yearbook.** Washington, DC: Broadcasting. (Annual)
Lists radio and television station, cable systems, satellites, advertising and marketing agencies, professional services, and consultants in the United States and Canada. The final section of the directory includes information on associations and education for broadcasting work.

150. **Burrelle's Media Directories.** Livingston, NJ: Burrelle. (Annual)
This company publishes state directories, primarily for northeastern states, and special directories for Black media, Hispanic media, and women's media.

151. **Cable TV Publicity Outlets Nationwide.** New Milford, CT: Public Relations Plus. (Semiannual)
Similar format to *All TV Publicity Outlets Nationwide* (entry 144).

152. Darnay, Brigitte, T., and Nimchuk, John, eds. **Newsletters Directory.** 3d ed. Detroit, MI: Gale, 1987. 1,162 p.
Includes over eight thousand U.S. publications—free, subscription, and membership newsletters, bulletins, etc. *National Directory of Newsletter and Reporting Services* was the title of previous editions.

153. **Editor and Publisher International Yearbook.** New York: Editor & Publisher. (Annual)
Lists daily and weekly newspapers of the United States and Canada and daily papers from other countries. Additional listings include syndicated services, equipment suppliers, foreign correspondents, organizations, and schools of journalism.

154. **Gale Directory of Publications: An Annual Guide to Newspapers, Magazines, Journals and Related Publications.** Detroit, MI: Gale. (Annual)
Formerly *Ayer's Directory*, this is a standard reference source for current information on American newspapers and serials. Arrangement is by city of publication.

155. **Gebbie Press All-in-One Directory**. New Paltz, NY: Gebbie. (Annual)
    Includes magazines, arranged by categories; radio and television stations; newspapers and syndicates; and special publications.

156. **Hudson's Washington News Media Contacts Directory**. Rhinebeck, NY: Newsletter Clearinghouse. (Annual with quarterly update.)
    A guide to the Washington, DC, press corps.

157. **International Directory of Special Events and Festivals**. Chicago: Special Events Reports. (Annual)
    The first edition (1984-85) covered approximately three thousand events.

158. Leonard, Margaret, ed. **Hudson's Newsletter Directory**. 6th ed. Rhinebeck, NY: Newsletter Clearinghouse, 1986. 385 p.
    Covers mostly English-language subscription newsletters; excludes free, irregular, and controlled-circulation publications. Also features a section titled "Newsletters, a Continuing History."

159. **National Directory of Weekly Newspapers**. Brooklyn, NY: American Newspaper Representatives. (Annual)
    Covers community newspapers in a geographic arrangement with advertising rates and circulation figures.

160. **National Radio Publicity Directory: The Publicists Radio Book**. New York: Peter Glenn. (Annual)
    Includes local, network, and syndicated shows, with program content; listings arranged by state.

161. Standard Rate and Data Service, Inc. **Print Media Editorial Calendars**. Business, consumer/farm, and newspaper editions. Wilmette, IL: SRDS. (Monthly)
    Entries include profile, personnel, types of editorial material accepted, regular departments and features, editorial emphasis, and circulation. SRDS also publishes a number of other directories useful in public relations work.

162. **Syndicated Columnists**. New York: Larimi. (Annual with monthly updates.)
    A directory listing over thirteen hundred columnists, with information about column content.

163. **TV News**. New York: Larimi. (Annual)
    Television news departments; local, regional, and national networks.

164. **Television Contacts**. New York: Larimi. (Annual with monthly updates.)
    Includes stations and syndicates that use guests or prepared copy.

165. Weiner, Richard. **News Bureaus in the United States**. New York: Public Relations Publishing. (Biennial)
    Provides information about five hundred bureaus maintained by newspapers, magazines, business publications, and wire services.

166. **The Working Press of the Nation.** 5 vols. Chicago: National Research Bureau. (Annual)

The five volumes cover newspapers; magazines; television and radio stations; feature writers and photographers; and internal publications. Gives names and titles of personnel. Indexes in each volume.

Directories of Public Relations Personnel

The following directories list persons and firms active in public relations and related work as well as organizations involved in lobbying and other types of promotional or special-interest activities. These directories generally provide, at a minimum, names, addresses, and affiliations; many of them also include useful information about corporations or organizations and their funding activities.

In this first listing are included individuals and firms whose primary activity is the practice of public relations in one or more of its aspects.

167. **National Directory of Corporate Public Affairs.** Washington, DC: Columbia. (Annual)

Includes corporate public affairs personnel by corporate and personal name and by industry. For each corporation, information is included about political action committees (PACs), foundations, and relevant publications.

168. **O'Dwyer's Directory of Corporate Communications.** New York: O'Dwyer. (Annual)

Includes corporations and trade associations, with names of communications personnel. Indexed by industry and geographic area.

169. **O'Dwyer's Directory of Public Relations Executives.** New York: O'Dwyer. (Every three years)

Provides detailed biographical information for corporate public relations executives.

170. **O'Dwyer's Directory of Public Relations Firms.** New York: O'Dwyer. (Annual)

Comprehensive listing of firms, many with account lists; indexed by clients, geographic location, and specialties. Also includes a ranked list of the fifty largest public relations firms.

171. Public Relations Society of America. **Register.** New York: PRSA. (Annual)

Published annually as the second September issue of *Public Relations Journal.* Members are listed by name, geographically, by organization names, and for sections of the PRSA. Recipients of PRSA awards (Gold and Silver Anvil Awards, Outstanding Educator Award, and Paul M. Lund Public Service Award) are also given, and the current text of the PRSA Code of Professional Standards is reproduced.

172. **Who's Who in Public Relations (International).** 6th ed. Meriden, NH: PR Publishing Company, 1984.

Includes educational background, positions held, memberships and awards; geographical index. (Fifth edition examined, 731 p.)

The next listing includes directories of lobbyists and political action committees. Because people and organizations enter and leave this field steadily, some of these sources are already out-of-date. An up-to-date list is published quarterly in *Congressional Record*.

173. **Directory of Business-Related Political Action Committees Registered with the Federal Election Commission**. Washington, DC: Business-Industry Political Action Committee, 1981. 137 p.

174. **Directory of Registered Lobbyists and Lobbyist Legislation**. 2d ed. Chicago: Marquis, 1975. 645 p.

Lobbyists are listed by state, with indexes by name and organization represented. Also included are federal and state laws relating to lobbying.

175. Greevy, David U.; Gore, Chadwick R.; and Weinberger, Marvin I., eds. **The PAC Directory**. 2d ed. 2 vol. Cambridge, MA: Ballinger, 1984. Vol. 1: 942 p.; Vol. 2: 873 p.

The 1984 edition covers the 1982 election cycle: volume 1 lists candidates, with funding received and ratings by Political Action Committees (PACs); volume 2 summarizes PAC finances and activities.

176. Roeder, Edward. **PACs Americana: A Directory of Political Action Committees (PACs) and Their Interests**. Washington, DC: Sunshine Services, 1982. 859 p.

Based on the 1979-80 elections, this work lists PACs by sponsoring organizations and by interest categories. Major financial contributions are given for a variety of candidate types, but no information on individual candidates is provided.

177. **Washington Representatives**. Washington, DC: Columbia. (Annual)

Directory of lobbyists, lawyers, and special-interest advocates in the nation's capital; data includes names of individuals and firms and who they represent. Indexed by subject and foreign interests.

Other Directories

Listed here are three directories for specific reference. One provides information about corporate sources of grants and the others index nonprofit organizations. These are provided as examples of the types of resources available for corporate and association information, a selection based on personal preference from the large number of directories available.

178. **National Trade and Professional Associations of the United States**. Washington, DC: Columbia. (Annual)

A comprehensive listing of trade, labor, professional, scientific, and technical organizations, with addresses, membership information, budget ranges, historical notes, and lists of their publications and annual meetings.

179. **Public Interest Profiles**. Washington, DC: Foundation for Public Affairs. (Biennial)

The 5th edition (1986-87) contains detailed information on 250 organizations, including third-party evaluations. In loose-leaf format with two or more pages of information for each organization.

180. Public Management Institute staff, comps. **Corporate 500: The Directory of Corporate Philanthropy**. 5th ed. Detroit, MI: Gale, 1986.

Lists corporations active in philanthropic giving, especially those without their own foundations. Information provided for each corporation is designed to aid grant seekers in identifying potential funding sources. The Public Management Institute (358 Brannan St., San Francisco, CA 94107) also has an extensive list of publications on fund raising, corporate giving, nonprofit management, and personnel and office management (*see* entry 131).

ORGANIZATIONS

The Public Relations Society of America is the major association in the United States for public relations practitioners, but it is only one of many organizations that represent the various aspects of public relations work. In addition, there are international public relations bodies, educational and research associations, and a large number of groups whose purpose is to influence and educate in the interest of their members.

Public Relations Practitioners

The major organizations of specific interest to public relations practitioners are listed here.

Agricultural Relations Council. 1629 K Street N.W., Suite 1100, Washington, DC 20006. Established 1953.

Members: employees of agricultural associations, agencies, and corporations involved in public relations.

Publications: *ARClight* (monthly); directory.

American Association of Fund-Raising Counsel. 25 W. 43rd St., New York, NY 10036. Established 1935.

Members: corporations.

Publications: *Fund-Raising Review* (biweekly); *Giving, USA* (annual).

American Association of Political Consultants. 202 E St., N.E., Washington, DC 20002. Established 1969.

Members: political campaign consultants.

Publications: *Newsletter* (quarterly).

American Society for Hospital Marketing and Public Relations (American Hospital Association). 840 N. Lake Shore Drive, Chicago, IL 60611. Established 1964. (Formerly American Society for Hospital Public Relations.)

Members: public relations workers in medical/health care fields.

Publications: *Hospital Marketing and Public Relations* (bimonthly).

American Society of Association Executives. 1575 Eye Street N.W., Washington, DC 20005. (Public Relations Division.) Established 1920.

Affiliated with: A-PAC, ASAE Foundation.

Members: executives of trade and other associations.

Publications: *Association Management* (monthly; entry 261); *Inside ASAE* (biweekly).

Association for Business Communication. English Building, University of Illinois, 608 S. Wright St., Urbana, IL 61801. (Formerly American Business Communication Association.) Established 1935.

Members: higher education faculty, business managers, and people engaged in business writing.

Publications: *Bulletin* (quarterly); *Journal of Business Communication* (quarterly; entry 217); monographs and bibliographies (for an example, refer to entry 272); annual directory.

Bank Marketing Association. 309 W. Washington St., Chicago, IL 60606. (Includes former Financial Public Relations Association.) Established 1915.

Members: marketing and public relations executives in banking.

Publications: *Bank Marketing* (monthly); *Community Bank Marketing Newsletter* (ten issues per year); *IC Newsletter* (quarterly); *Resource* (semimonthly).

Confederation Europeenne des Relations Publiques (European Confederation of Public Relations). 12, avenue du Ront-Point, B-1330 Rixensort, Belgium. Established 1959.

Members: national public relations associations and individual consultants.

Publications: *CERP Newsletter* (monthly); conference proceedings; *CERP Directory* (annual).

Council for Advancement and Support of Education (CASE). Suite 400, 11 Dupont Circle, Washington, DC 20036. Established 1974.

Members: educational institutions and individuals involved in managing institutional advancement and public relations programs.

Publications: *Currents* (monthly; entry 263).

Institute of Public Relations. Gate House, St. John's Square, London EC1M 4DH, England. Established 1948.

Members: British public relations practitioners from government and the private sector.

Publications. *Public Relations* (quarterly) (entry 197). *See also* entry 456.

International Association of Business Communicators. 870 Market St., Suite 940, San Francisco, CA 94102. Established 1970.

Affiliated with: IABC Foundation.

Members: communication managers in business and nonprofit organizations (and self-employed), mainly responsible for employee communications.

Publications: *Communication World* (monthly except July; entry 193); *IABC Update* (quarterly); occasional monographs; also provides handbooks, samples of publications, and videotapes on request for members. Sponsors annual Gold Quill awards, encourages local and student chapters, and offers accreditation for business communicators. *See also* entry 369.

International Communication Association. Box 9589, Austin, TX 78766. Established 1950.

Members: academics with interest in communication theory.

Publications: *Communication Yearbook* (annual); *Human Communication Research* (quarterly; entry 215); *ICA Newsletter* (quarterly); bibliography (entry 272).

International Public Relations Association. Case Postale 126, CH-1211 Geneva 20, Switzerland. Established 1955.

Affiliated with: International Foundation for Public Relations Research and Education.

Members: public relations executives worldwide.

Publications: *International Public Relations Review* (quarterly, entry 194) and *IPRA Newsletter* (bimonthly).

This body sponsors and publishes a Gold Paper series consisting of papers presented at the World Public Relations Congress. A pertinent title in this series is *Public Relations and Propaganda: Values Compared* by Tim Traverse-Healy (Gold Paper no. 6, 1988; 24 p.). *See also* entry 183.

Issue Management Association. 1110 Vermont Ave. N.W., Suite 1150, Washington, DC 20005. Established 1982.

Members: corporate and government executives.

Publications: *Issue Managers' Newsletter* (monthly).

Library Public Relations Council. 15 Park Row, Suite 434, New York, NY 10017. Established 1939.

Members: library public relations directors.

Publications: acts as a clearinghouse. No regular publications.

National Association of Government Communicators. 80 S. Early St., Alexandria, VA 22304. Established 1976.

Members: government public information and communications officers.

Publications: *Journal of Public Communication* (annual); *NAGC Communicator* (monthly).

National Council for Community Relations. 1987 address: c/o Mark Olson, P.O. Box 69, Greeley, CO 80632. (No permanent address.) Established 1974.

Members: public relations personnel in junior and community colleges.

Publications: *Counsel* (quarterly).

National Investor Relations Institute. 1730 M Street N.W., Suite 806, Washington, DC 20036. Established 1967.

Members: corporate officers and investor relations consultants.

Publications: *Investor Relations Update* (monthly; entry 205); directories.

National School Public Relations Association. 1501 Lee Highway, Arlington, VA 22209. Established 1935.

Members: educators, members of trade organizations, government officials.

Publications: *Education USA* (weekly); *It Starts in the Classroom* (monthly).

National Society of Fund Raising Executives. 1101 King St., Suite 3000, Alexandria, VA 22314. Established 1960.

Members: individuals in fund raising positions.

Publications: *NSFRE News* (ten issues per year); *Journal* (biennial).

Public Affairs Council. 1255 23rd Street N.W., Suite 750, Washington, DC 20037. Established 1954.

Affiliated with: Foundation for Public Affairs.

Members: corporate sponsors.

Publications: *Impact* (monthly); *Perspectives* (quarterly); *Public Affairs Review* (annual; entry 196).

Public Relations Society of America. 845 Third Ave., New York, NY 10022. Established 1948.

Affiliated with: Foundation for Public Relations Research and Education; Public Relations Student Society of America; Accrediting Council on Education in Journalism and Mass Communication.

Members: public relations executives, counselors, and other practitioners.

Publications: *Public Relations Journal* (monthly; entry 198); *Register* (annual issue of *Public Relations Journal*; entry 171); *Bibliography for Public Relations Professionals* (entry 278); special reports.

Supports fourteen special-interest sections for practitioners in various fields; also has a district and chapter substructure. Local chapters sponsor workshops and forums for continuing education. Maintains an information center and career referral service for members. Sponsors Silver and Gold Anvil awards for recognition of outstanding public relations programs and individuals, Bronze Anvil award for film and video productions, and other awards for outstanding educators and public service activities.

Public Utilities Communicators Association. 122 Decker Dr., New Castle, PA 16105. Established 1922.

Members: executives and public relations specialists for public utilities.

Publications: *Newsletter; PUCA Communicator/Showcase* (quarterly).

Railroad Public Relations Association. American Railroads Building, Washington, DC 20036. Established 1952.

Members: railroad public relations executives.

Publications: *Interline* (bimonthly).

Religious Public Relations Council. 475 Riverside Dr., New York, NY 10027. Established 1929.

Members: public relations practitioners serving religious organizations.

Publications: *The Counselor* (quarterly).

Society of Consumer Affairs Professionals in Business. 4900 Leesburg Pike, Suite 311, Alexandria, VA 22302. Established 1973.

Affiliated with: SOCAP Foundation.

Members: consumer relations executives.

Publications: *Mobius* (biennial); *Update* (monthly).

State Governmental Affairs Council. 1001 Connecticut Ave. N.W., Suite 800, Washington, DC 20036. Established 1975.

    Members: major corporations engaged in interstate commerce.

    Publications: *SGAC News* (eight issues per year).

Women Executives in Public Relations. Box 781, Murray Hill Station, New York, NY 10156. Established 1946.

    Members: women in public relations.

Women in Communications. Box 9561, Austin, TX 78766. Established 1909.

    Members: women in communications.

    Publications: *The Professional Communicator* (bimonthly).

Women in Government Relations. 1311-A Dolly Madison Blvd., McLean, VA 22101. Established 1975.

    Members: women in public affairs and government relations.

    Publications: *Newsletter* (monthly).

Educational and Research Organizations

    The following list of organizations includes accrediting and primarily educational bodies.

Accrediting Council on Education in Journalism and Mass Communication. (Formerly American Council on Education for Journalism.) School of Journalism, University of Kansas, Lawrence, KS 66045. Established 1945.

    Accrediting body for communication, journalism, and public relations programs in higher education.

American Association for Public Opinion Research. P.O. Box 17, Princeton, NJ 08542. Established 1947.

    Concerned with the methods and applications of public opinion and social research. Holds an annual conference.

    Publications: *Public Opinion Quarterly* (quarterly; entry 235); *AAPOR News* (three times a year).

American Political Science Association. 1527 New Hampshire Ave. N.W., Washington, DC 20036. Established 1903.

    Membership includes educators, businessmen, public officials, and other interested persons. Through research and educational programs, promotes the study of the art and science of government.

    Publications: *American Political Science Review* (quarterly; entry 229); *PS: News for Teachers of Political Science* (quarterly; *see also* entry 291). Holds annual conference.

Association for Education in Journalism and Mass Communication. University of South Carolina, Columbia, SC. Established 1912. (Public Relations Division.)

Publications: *AEJMC News* (ten issues per year); *Journalism Abstracts* (annual; entry 295); *Journalism Educator* (quarterly; entry 219); *Journalism Monographs* (entry 220); *JQ: Journalism Quarterly* (entry 296); *Mass Comm Review* (irregular; entry 221); annual directory. Holds annual conference.

Institute for Public Relations Research and Education. 310 Madison Ave., Suite 1816, New York, NY 10017. Established 1956 as Foundation for Public Relations Research and Education (through 1988).

Publications: founded and published volumes 1-13 of *Public Relations Review* (quarterly; entry 200); *Public Relations Bibliography* (annual; entry 282); annual report; monographs.

Sponsors student competitions and scholarships, awards, surveys and lectures. In 1988, the institute announced that it plans to produce a new serial publication, at an unspecified future date, for public relations practitioners.

Public Relations Student Society of America. c/o PRSA, 845 Third Ave., New York, NY 10022.

Affiliated with: Public Relations Society of America.

Members: college and university students.

Publications: *Forum* (quarterly).

Business and Interest-Group Organizations

This list includes some of the major industrial and professional associations, all of which are actively engaged in public relations activities on behalf of their constituencies or members. The specific publications of these organizations have not been listed here, but they can be found in *National Trade and Professional Associations of the United States* (entry 178).

American Bankers Association. 1120 Connecticut Ave. N.W., Washington, DC 20036. Established 1875.

American Business Conference. 1730 K Street N.W., Suite 703, Washington, DC 20006. Established 1980.

American Chemical Society. 1155 16th Street N.W., Washington, DC 20036. Established 1876.

American Council of Life Insurance. 1850 K Street N.W., Washington, DC 20006. Established 1939 under earlier name.

American Dairy Association and Dairy Council, Inc. 6300 N. River Rd., Rosemont, IL 60018. Established 1940.

American Medical Association. 535 N. Dearborn St., Chicago, IL 60610. Established 1847.

American Petroleum Institute. 1220 L Street N.W., Washington, DC 20005. Established 1919.

American Pharmaceutical Association. 2215 Constitution Ave. N.W., Washington, DC 20037. Established 1852.

Business Roundtable. 200 Park Ave., New York, NY 10166. Established 1972.

Chamber of Commerce of the United States. 1613 H Street N.W., Washington, DC 20062. Established 1912.

Chemical Manufacturers Association. 2501 M Street N.W., Washington, DC 20037. Established 1872.

Insurance Information Institute. 110 William St., New York, NY 10038. Established 1959.

National Association of Home Builders. 15th and M Streets N.W., Washington, DC 20005. Established 1942.

National Association of Manufacturers. 1776 F Street N.W., Washington, DC 20006. Established 1895.

National Rifle Association of America. 1600 Rhode Island Ave. N.W., Washington, DC 20036. Established 1871.

Technical Association of the Pulp and Paper Industry. Box 105113, Technology Park, Atlanta, GA 30348. Established 1915.

Tobacco Institute. 1875 Eye Street N.W., Suite 800, Washington, DC 20006. Established 1958.

Other Organizations

Arts and Business Council. 130 E. 40th St., New York, NY 10016.
Established in 1973 to act as liaison between the arts and business communities, assisting corporations with public relations and community involvement programs and instructing arts organizations in management techniques and responsiveness to business needs. Produces semiannual and annual publications.

Business Committee for the Arts. 1775 Broadway, Suite 510, New York, NY 10019.

An organization of business leaders, founded in 1967, to encourage business support of the arts. Manages a national public service advertising campaign and an awards program.

Publishes *BCA News* (bimonthly); books and pamphlets.

Center for Corporate Public Involvement. 1850 K Street N.W., Washington, DC.

Established in 1971 as the Clearinghouse for Corporate Social Responsibility, and sponsored by insurance associations, this organization assists insurance companies in their public affairs work.

Publishes *Response* (quarterly) and *Social Report* (annual).

Council on Economic Priorities. 30 Irving Place, New York, NY 10003.

Founded in 1969 and supported largely by foundation grants, this organization provides information on corporate human-service and consumer-directed activities and develops criteria for assessing corporate performance in these areas.

Publications include a monthly newsletter, reports, and studies.

Foundation for Economic Education. 30 S. Broadway, Irvington-on-Hudson, NY 10533.

Founded in 1946 and supported by business foundations, this organization provides research and services in support of the free enterprise economic system. It produces material for high schools and colleges and sponsors public education programs.

Publishes *The Freeman* (monthly).

A program with a similar mission is Business in the Classroom, sponsored by the Constitutional Rights Foundation, Greer, SC.

The Media Institute. 3017 M. Street N.W., Washington, DC 20007.

Founded in 1976 and funded by foundation and corporate grants, this organization's stated purpose is the improvement of business and economic news coverage and promotion of a strong free press.

Publishes short studies on such topics as media treatment of inflation (1980), the businessman's image (1981) and artificial sweeteners (1986); also publishes *Business and the Media* (three times a year) and *Media Institute Forum* (quarterly).

National Association of Broadcasters. 1771 N Street N.W., Washington, DC 20036.

An organization of station and network representatives. One of its functions is to help organizations adopt appropriate approaches to the media.

Pamphlets published by NAB include *If You Want Free Air Time* and *So You're Going on TV*. Regular publications are *Highlights* (weekly) and *Radioactive* (monthly).

EDUCATION FOR PUBLIC RELATIONS

Where public relations is an identifiable program in college and university sequences, the programs are listed in such standard guides to higher education as *The College Blue Book*. The Public Relations Society of America, the Public Relations Division of the Association for Education in Journalism and Mass Communication, the International Public

Relations Association, and the Institute for Public Relations Research and Education are active in disseminating information about the current status of public relations education and preparing models for improving the educational sequence. In addition, articles relating to education for public relations appear regularly in *Public Relations Journal, Public Relations Quarterly* and *Public Relations Review* (entries 198, 199, and 200, respectively).

Academic programs in public relations that lead to a degree specialization or major are generally limited to schools of journalism and/or communication. This is a source of concern to some public relations leaders because the management-advisory aspects of public relations may be slighted in this discipline; however, the communications context is well established, and public relations sequences are accredited (with representation from PRSA) by the Accrediting Council on Education in Journalism and Mass Communication.

Recent studies from these bodies include the following titles:

181. **Advancing Public Relations Education.** New York: Institute for Public Relations Research and Education (for the Commission on Public Relations Education, the Association for Education in Journalism and Mass Communication, and the Public Relations Society of America), 1985. 12 p.

Guidelines for graduate-level education in the field.

182. **A Design for Public Relations Education.** New York: Public Relations Society of America (for the Commission on Undergraduate Public Relations Education, the Public Relations Division of the Association for Education in Journalism and Mass Communication, and the Education Section, Public Relations Society of America), 1987. 33 p.

Guidelines for undergraduate education. Available from PRSA. (Not examined.)

183. **A Model for Public Relations Education for Professional Practice.** IPRA Gold Paper no. 4. London: International Public Relations Association's Education and Research Committee, 1982. 41 p.

Based on the "Hong Kong Document" drawn up in 1980 by an IPRA educators' group, this report recommends graduate-level preparation for public relations, faculty with both academic and professional credentials, and more research in the field.

184. Walker, Albert. **Public Relations Body of Knowledge. Sequences and Courses in United States Colleges and Universities.** New York: Institute for Public Relations Research and Education, 1988. 100 p.; bibliographies.

A recent publication of the institute, this work for practitioners provides an explanation of the theoretical bases of public relations. Included are lists of educational programs, online databases, and other professional resources.

185. Walker, Albert. **Status and Trends of Public Relations Education in United States Senior Colleges and Universities.** New York: Institute for Public Relations Research and Education, 1975. 2d ed. 1981.

1975 edition available as ERIC document 146600; 1981 edition available from the institute. Out of date but of historical value.

A list of accredited programs in public relations in institutions of higher education is available from the Public Relations Society of America for a nominal fee (currently one dollar). Apply to Career Information, Public Relations Society of America, 845 Third Ave., New York, NY 10022.

Current U.S. college and university programs in public relations include the following:

Ball State University (also Ph.D. program)

Boston University (established first Masters' program in public relations in 1947)

Bowling Green State University

California State University, Fullerton

Kent State University

Northwestern University, Medill School of Journalism

Ohio State University

Ohio University

Oklahoma State University (also Ph.D. program)

San Jose State University

Southern Mississippi State (also Ph.D. program)

Syracuse University, School of Public Communications (also Ph.D. program)

University of Alabama, School of Communication (also Ph.D. program)

University of Florida, Department of Advertising and Public Relations

University of Georgia, Henry W. Grady School of Journalism and Mass
    Communication

University of Maryland, College of Journalism

University of Northern Illinois

University of Oklahoma

University of Oregon

University of South Florida

University of Southern California, School of Journalism (also Ph.D. program)

University of Tennessee (also Ph.D. program)

University of Texas, Department of Journalism (also Ph.D. program)

University of Utah (also Ph.D. program)

University of Wisconsin-Madison, School of Journalism and Mass Communication
    (also Ph.D. program)

CAREER GUIDANCE

This section includes a selection of books and pamphlets that give information on public relations careers for students and school counselors, beginners in the field, and practitioners seeking guidance on advancing their careers.

186.   Bernays, Edward L. **Your Future in a Public Relations Career**. rev. ed. New York: Rosen Publishing Group, 1983. 146 p. bibliography.
   An introduction to the public relations field by one of its early educators and longtime practitioners. Bernays discusses educational and other qualifications, employment opportunities, and entry strategies. Appendices provide lists of associations, publications, and educational programs.

187.   Cole, Robert S. **Practical Handbook of Public Relations**. Englewood Cliffs, NJ: Prentice-Hall, 1981. 213 p. bibliography.
   An overview of public relations functions written specifically for students and beginners, with sections on entering the field.

188.   Druck, Kalman B., and Hiebert, Ray E. **Professional Development Guide**. rev. ed. New York: PRSA, 1984. 20 p.
   A continuing education guide for people already in the field, describing four career levels and suggesting skill-building resources. (Not examined.)

189.   Fry, Ronald W., ed. **Internships. Volume 1: Advertising, Marketing, Public Relations**. Hawthorne, NJ: Career Press, 1988. 253 p.
   Lists agencies that accept interns and offers general guidance to students. Reviewed in Fall 1988 issue of *Public Relations Review*. (Not examined.)

190.   Mainstream Access, Inc. **The Public Relations Job Finder**. Englewood Cliffs, NJ: Prentice-Hall, 1981. 190 p. bibliography.
   A general guide for job seekers and school counselors that includes a variety of useful material (based on Conference Board and PRSA sources) and a listing of resources for further information.

191.   **Public Relations Career Directory**. Career Directory Series. New York: Career Publishing Corporation. (Annual since 1986.)
   A comprehensive guide for entry-level job seekers. Consists of practical descriptions of work in various public relations specializations along with special skills needed, entry opportunities, and advancement and salary information. Prepared with the assistance of the Public Relations Society of America, the Institute for Public Relations Research and Education, and the public relations executives who contributed chapters. The final section of the work covers general job-search considerations, including preparation of resumes, interviewing techniques, and a listing of current entry-level positions and internships available in corporations, associations, and public relations agencies.

192.   Rotman, Morris. **Opportunities in Public Relations**. Lincolnwood, IL: VGM Career Horizons, 1983. 149 p. bibliography.

Ray E. Hiebert, who reviewed this work for *Public Relations Review* (Autumn 1984), states that it should be in high school and college guidance-center collections.

3

Research Tools

This chapter describes bibliographies and resources that appear in periodical, ongoing, or serial form. These sources and tools will lead students and other researchers into the rich body of current writing by public relations practitioners; scholars in communications, political science, marketing, and other disciplines; and observers of the corporate scene. Journals and other periodical publications are listed first, followed by bibliographies, printed indexes, online databases, and finally, a few useful publishers' series.

PERIODICALS

Because public relations originated in the discipline of communication but operates in the areas of business and political science, relevant articles can be found in the periodical and journal literature of all three areas. In addition, there is a core group of journals that focus narrowly on the public relations function. These journals are listed below, followed by the major newsletters published for public relations practitioners.

Public Relations Journals

193. **Communication World**. San Francisco, CA: International Association of Business Communicators. (Monthly except July.)

The membership journal of this association. Contains news of corporate public relations practitioners and executives. Most articles emphasize practical communication techniques but some discuss general topics and current trends. Includes book reviews and case studies.

194. **International Public Relations Review**. Geneva; International Public Relations Association. (Quarterly)

Short articles on public relations in other countries, topics of cross-national interest, surveys, and editorial opinion, with an occasional in-depth article. Also published for members of this association: *IPRA Newsletter* (bimonthly).

195. **Journal of Educational Public Relations**. Camp Hill, PA: Educational Communication Center. (Quarterly)

Short, practical articles and case studies for school administrators. Includes book reviews. Contents indexed annually by author and subject.

196. **Public Affairs Review**. Washington, DC: Public Affairs Council. (Annual)
Articles on contemporary issues in public and government relations written for corporate public affairs officers. Includes book reviews.

197. **Public Relations**. Harlow, England: Longman. (Quarterly)
Membership journal of the Institute of Public Relations. Includes book reviews. Published for practitioners in the United Kingdom.

198. **Public Relations Journal**. New York: PRSA. (Monthly)
The official membership journal of the society and an important resource for keeping abreast of events in the field. Includes two or three feature articles and one or more book reviews per issue. Register issue published annually.

199. **Public Relations Quarterly**. Rhinebeck, NY: Public Relations Quarterly. (Quarterly)
A basic resource for public relations practitioners, with a somewhat narrower, more practical orientation than *Public Relations Journal* (entry 198). Includes short articles (with authors' photographs), regular columns, and a few book reviews per issue.

200. **Public Relations Review: A Journal of Research and Comment**. Silver Spring, MD: Communication Research Associates, for the Institute for Public Relations Research and Education. (Quarterly)
The basic scholarly journal in the field (in fact, the only publication of this type since the short-lived [published Winter 1984 through Summer 1985] *Public Relations Research and Education*); includes reports of research, book reviews, and an annual bibliography (entry 282). An essential resource for monitoring research and new publications.

Note: A new publication, *Public Relations Research Annual* (Lawrence Erlbaum Assocs., Hillsdale, NJ), is scheduled to appear in 1989.

Newsletters for Practitioners

201. **Corporate Communications Report**. New York: Corporate Annual Reports, Inc. (Quarterly; approximately six pages per issue.)
A newsletter for executives in corporate communications and investor relations. Includes reports on surveys and practical tips.

202. **Corporate Public Issues and Their Management**. Stamford, CT: Issue Action Publications. (Semimonthly; approximately six pages per issue.)
Newsletter on issue management, reporting on new publications, developments in higher education, and corporate public affairs activities.

203. **Hi-Tech Alert for the Professional Communicator**. Silver Spring, MD: Communication Research Associates. (Monthly; four pages per issue.)
Reports on applications of current electronic technology for public relations practice.

204. **Investor Relations Newsletter**. Chicago: Enterprise Publications. (Monthly; four pages per issue)
Subtitled *A Monthly Letter Reporting on New Ideas, Trends and Problem Solving in the Field of Investor Relations*. Contents indexed annually. Includes book reviews.

205. **Investor Relations Update**. Washington, DC: National Investor Relations Institute. (Monthly; approximately twelve pages per issue.)
Short reports on corporate and regulatory developments and topics of interest in investor relations.

206. **Jack O'Dwyer's Newsletter**. New York: O'Dwyer. (Weekly; approximately six page per issue.)
News on personnel, corporate events, acquisitions, campaigns, and new publications and services in the field.

207. **O'Dwyer's PR Services Report**. New York: O'Dwyer. (Monthly; approximately forty pages per issue.)
New in 1987, this publication focuses on public relations services, including those made possible by new technology, such as video news releases, satellite media tours, and use of computer software.

208. **PR News**. New York: Public Relations News. (Weekly; four pages per issue.)
Established in 1944 by Denny Griswold, one of the important figures in the field, this newsletter features information about personnel, jobs, firms, and corporate public relations, including foreign and international programs. Occasional special reports also published for subscribers.

209. **PR Reporter: The Weekly Newsletter of Public Relations, Public Affairs & Communication**. Exeter, NH: PR Publishing Company. (Weekly; four pages per issue plus occasional supplements.)
A newsletter for public relations practitioners that includes news, reports of conferences and new publications, research findings, practical tips, and short articles. Regular supplements include "Managing the Human Climate," by Philip Lesly; "Purview," by Otto Lerbinger; and "Tips and Tactics." A special annual issue surveys salaries and summarizes issues in the field. Contents indexed semiannually.

210. **Ragan Report**. Chicago: Lawrence Ragan Communications. (Weekly; four pages per issue.)
Ideas and techniques for improving organizational publications plus news from the field.

211. **Social Science Monitor for Public Relations and Advertising Executives**. Silver Spring, MD: Communication Research Associates. (Monthly; four pages per issue.)
Provides abstracts of current social-science research. Edited by Ray E. Hiebert, former Dean of the University of Maryland College of Journalism.

212. **Video Monitor: Report on Television Developments for Public Communicators**. Silver Spring, MD: Communication Research Associates. (Monthly; four pages per issue.)
Summaries of research and new developments in television and related technology.

For purposes of this book, scholarly journals have been sorted into the disciplines of communication, business, and political science. A fourth list consists of a few journals that do not fit into these three categories but contain material of relevance to public relations.

Scholarly Journals in Journalism
and Communication

213. Communication Research: An International Quarterly. Newbury Park, CA: Sage. (Quarterly)

Studies of the media and other communication topics. Some issues include review essays. Contents indexed annually by author and title.

214. Gazette: International Journal for Mass Communication Studies. Dordrecht, Netherlands: Nijhoff. (Three issues per year.)

A journal of scholarly articles of international scope with occasional book reviews and bibliographies. Contents are grouped under the broad headings of Press/Radio/Television, Propaganda/Public Opinion, and Advertising/Public Relations. Limited application to public relations practice.

215. Human Communication Research. Newbury Park, CA: Sage. (Quarterly)

Official journal of the International Communication Association. Contents indexed annually by author and title.

216. Journal of Broadcasting and Electronic Media. Kent, OH: Broadcast Education Association. (Quarterly)

Formerly *Journal of Broadcasting*, this publication includes articles, book review essays, and short reviews. Contents indexed annually by author and title.

217. Journal of Business Communication. Urbana, IL: Association for Business Communication. (Quarterly)

Emphasis is on writing and speaking skills. Includes book reviews and a review essay in each issue. Contents indexed annually by author, title, and subject.

218. Journal of Communication. Philadelphia, PA: Annenberg School of Communications, University of Pennsylvania, in cooperation with the National Society for the Study of Communication. (Quarterly)

Many articles relevant to public relations. Substantial book review section in each issue. Contents indexed annually by author and title.

219. Journalism Educator. Columbia, SC: Association for Education in Journalism and Mass Communication. (Quarterly)

Includes an annual directory of schools of journalism and mass communications in the United States.

220. Journalism Monographs. Columbia, SC: Association for Education in Journalism and Mass Communication. (Irregular)

Each issue consists of a single article and its bibliography. Several issues on topics related to public relations.

221. Mass Comm Review. Columbia, SC: Mass Communications and Society Division, Association for Education in Journalism and Mass Communication. (Irregular: one to three issues per year.)

Scholarly articles on journalism topics, including political communication.

Scholarly Journals in Business, Management, and Marketing

222. **Academy of Management Journal**. Mississippi State, MS: Academy of Management. (Quarterly)
Articles on management topics with a practical slant. Contents indexed annually by author, title, and subject.

223. **Business and Society Review**. Boston: Warren, Gorham & Lamont. (Quarterly)
Focuses on business-government relationships and corporate social responsibility. Special features include company performance roundup in each issue and an annual survey of poor public relations practices. Includes book reviews.

224. **California Management Review**. Berkeley, CA: Graduate School of Business Administration, University of California. (Quarterly)
Topics include corporate political activity and social issues in management. Includes book reviews. Contents indexed annually by author, title, and subject.

225. **Harvard Business Review**. Boston: Graduate School of Business Administration, Harvard University. (Bimonthly)
Includes many articles on business-government relations, corporate social responsibility and image building, and other topics relevant to public relations. Contents indexed annually by author and subject; cumulative self-indexing also. Online version available (entry 311).

226. **Journal of Advertising**. Athens, GA: American Academy of Advertising. (Quarterly)
Research articles; includes book reviews. Contents indexed every five years by author and subject.

227. **Journal of Marketing**. Chicago: American Marketing Association. (Quarterly)
Includes book reviews and a review of recent marketing periodical literature in each issue. Contents indexed annually by author and subject.

228. **Research in Corporate Social Performance and Policy**. Greenwich, CT: Jai Press. (Annual)
Research studies and surveys with bibliographies.

Scholarly Journals in Political Science

229. **American Political Science Review**. Washington, DC: American Political Science Association. (Quarterly)
Includes articles on political communication; extensive book reviews.

230. **American Politics Quarterly**. Newbury Park, CA: Sage. (Quarterly)
Useful for political public relations material. Contents indexed annually by author and title.

231. **Journal of Politics**. Gainesville, FL: Southern Political Science Association. (Quarterly)
Includes a large section of book reviews and a review essay in each issue. Contents indexed annually by author.

232. **Political Communication and Persuasion: An International Journal**. New York: Crane, Russak. (Quarterly)
Topics include government public information offices, campaign practices, and foreign-government public relations activities. Many articles on conditions in foreign countries. Contents indexed annually by author and title.

233. **Political Communication Bulletin**. Published monthly 1965-1975 by the American Institute for Political Communication, Washington, DC.
A small publication (six to eight pages), the purpose of which was to give news and analysis of contemporary politics from the communications perspective. Topics included legislative actions, presidential public relations, media attitudes toward candidates, opinion polls, and analyses of the communications aspects of political actions.

234. **Presidential Studies Quarterly**. New York: Center for the Study of the Presidency. (Quarterly)
Articles on political communication topics. Includes book reviews. Contents indexed annually by author.

235. **Public Opinion Quarterly**. Princeton, NJ: American Association for Public Opinion Research. (Quarterly)
Reports of recent polls and articles on opinion research and topical issues. Includes a few book reviews per issue.

236. **Western Political Quarterly**. Salt Lake City, UT: Western Political Science Association and the Political Science Associations of Southern California, Northern California, and the Pacific Northwest. (Quarterly)
Contents indexed annually by author.

Other Scholarly Journals

237. **American Journal of Sociology**. Chicago: University of Chicago Press. (Bimonthly)
Basic sociological title; includes book reviews.

238. **Journal of Personality and Social Psychology**. Arlington, VA: American Psychological Association. (Quarterly)
Content of each issue is organized in three major sections: attitudes and social cognition; interpersonal relations and group processes; and personality. No book reviews. Contents indexed annually by author only.

239. **Journal of Social Issues**. Ann Arbor, MI: Society for the Psychological Study of Social Issues. (Quarterly)
Focus is social psychology, with a special topic for each issue. No book reviews.

The so-called popular periodicals, intended for members of specific industry groups as well as students and the general public, contain material of interest in the study of public relations – sometimes documenting its effects and sometimes examining the practice itself in a particular context. These periodicals have been divided by subject into three groups: journalism and the media, business and marketing, and nonprofit organization management.

Journalism and Media Magazines

240. **Broadcasting**. Washington, DC: Broadcasting. (Weekly)
News of commercial television and radio for members of the broadcasting industry. Also publishes the annual *Broadcasting/Cablecasting Yearbook* (entry 149).

241. **Channels of Communications**. New York: Media Commentary Council. (Bimonthly)
Articles by journalists and journalism educators on the television medium for members of the industry, students, and the general public. Some book reviews included.

242. **Columbia Journalism Review**. New York: Columbia University, Graduate School of Journalism. (Bimonthly)
Articles by scholars and journalists on a range of media-related topics. Includes book reviews.

243. **EC & TJ: Educational Communication and Technology Journal**. Washington, DC: Association for Educational Communications and Technology. (Quarterly)
News and articles of interest to educators and communications specialists. Includes book reviews.

244. **Editor and Publisher: The Fourth Estate**. New York: Editor & Publisher. (Weekly)
The trade publication of the newspaper press. Frequent articles on political aspects of reporting. Also publishes *Editor and Publisher International Yearbook* (entry 153).

245. **Quill**. Chicago: Society of Professional Journalists/Sigma Delta Thi. (Eleven issues per year.)
A trade publication for journalists, with notes and articles on practical aspects of journalistic work; also features news and awards.

246. **Washington Journalism Review (WJR)**. Washington, DC: WJR. (Ten issues per year.)
Popular coverage of the news media, with emphasis on political topics. Includes book reviews.

Business and Marketing Magazines

247. **ABA Banking Journal**. Bristol, CT: Simmons-Boardman. (Monthly)
Includes articles on public relations aspects of banking.

248. **Across the Board**. New York: Conference Board. (Eleven issues per year.)
Includes book reviews. Annual subject index covers this title and all other Conference Board serial publications (*see* entry 324).

249. **Advertising Age**. Chicago: Crain. (Weekly)
Includes book reviews. Many special features, including corporate-image advertising, agency income, marketing, and advertising research.

250. **Business Marketing**. Chicago: Crain. (Monthly)
Special features include best trade-show exhibits. Includes book reviews.

251. **Business Week**. New York: McGraw-Hill. (Weekly)
Various special issues; includes book reviews.

252. **Financial Analysts' Journal**. New York: Financial Analysts Federation. (Bimonthly)
Topics include corporate reporting practices and SEC regulations. Includes book reviews. Contents indexed annually by author.

253. **Fortune**. New York: Time, Inc. (Biweekly)
Various special features and issues; includes book reviews.

254. **Institutional Investor**. New York: Institutional Investor. (Monthly)
Features include a regular investor-relations article and annual selection of best corporate annual reports. One book review per issue.

255. **Marketing Communications**. New York: United Business Publications. (Monthly)
Special issues feature lists of sporting events with corporate sponsorship, sales-promotion agencies, and other topics of interest in marketing.

256. **Public Opinion**. Washington, DC: American Enterprise Institute for Public Policy Research. (Bimonthly)
Features include opinion roundup.

257. **Sales and Marketing Management**. New York: Bill Communications. (Sixteen issues per year.)
Special issues, including awards winners. Includes book reviews.

258. **Social Issues Service: News for Investors**. Washington, DC: Investor Responsibility Research Center (IRRC). (Eleven issues per year.)
Reports on current shareholder-activism issues.

259. **Social Issues Service: Proxy Issues Report**. Washington, DC: Investor Responsibility Research Center (IRRC). (Irregular)
Reports on issues raised by shareholders for inclusion on proxy ballots.

Magazines for Nonprofit Organization Managers

260. **Association and Society Manager**. Los Angeles: Brentwood. (Bimonthly)
Addresses practical concerns of managers. Includes book reviews.

261. **Association Management**. Washington, DC: American Society of Association Executives. (Monthly)
Articles on topics such as convention planning and publicity, membership campaigns, lobbying, and other public relations areas.

262. **Association Trends**. Bethesda, MD: Martineau. (Weekly)
Practical ideas for association executives. Includes book reviews.

263. **Currents**. Washington, DC: Council for Advancement and Support of Education. (Monthly)
Short- to medium-length articles on institutional-advancement topics. Includes CASE recognition awards as well as directories of professional services and suppliers. Annual author, title, and subject indexes.

264. **Foundation News: The Magazine of Philanthropy**. Washington, DC: Council on Foundations. (Bimonthly)
Written for executives of private foundations. Articles on topics such as annual-report preparation and influencing public policy making. Includes book reviews.

265. **Fund Raising Management**. Garden City, NY: Hoke. (Monthly)
Information for development directors and other nonprofit executives. Contents indexed annually by title. Also publishes *FRM Weekly*.

BIBLIOGRAPHIES

Interest in the literature of public relations has grown as the practice has grown. In the late 1940s and early 1950s, the first bibliographies on the subject appeared in a series edited by William A. Nielander and published by the Bureau of Business Research at the University of Texas. During the 1950s and 1960s, Scott M. Cutlip authored for the University of Wisconsin Press the first edition of a reference list that was to appear regularly thereafter under various auspices (*see* entries 267 and 282). In 1970, Alice Norton's bibliography (entry 277) was issued; that publication date provides the starting point for selection of most of the entries in this volume.

During the later 1970s and especially in the 1980s, two types of bibliographic works appeared. Some treat public relations within the context of other subjects, such as fund raising, political campaigning, and marketing, while others focus on public relations in particular settings, such as municipal government, police departments, and corporations. The only compilation since Norton's that approaches comprehensive coverage of the subject is the annual list sponsored by the Institute for Public Relations Research and Education and formerly published in the Winter issue of *Public Relations Review* (*see* entry 282). This bibliography, compiled since 1977 by Albert Walker, represents the continuation of Cutlip's project, which was taken up by Robert L. Bishop in 1974 after the second edition in 1965 of Cutlip's original pioneering work.

In 1988, a group operating under the auspices of the Public Relations Society of America made a new effort to organize the literature of public relations. The first list of readings from the Public Relations Body of Knowledge Task Force appeared in the Spring 1988 issue of *Public Relations Review*. This listing, including books, pamphlets, and journal articles, is organized in six categories that represent the critical aspects of public relations as determined by the task force. Topic headings are foundations of public relations, organizational and managerial contexts, communications and relationship contexts, processes, professional practice, and contexts of professional practice. It is reported this bibliography will be edited and expanded at a later date; its initial appearance is marked by unnecessary duplication and imperfect editing. Nevertheless, it represents a commendable attempt to develop a highly selective guide to this body of knowledge. The Institute for Public Relations Research and Education has also addressed this topic (*see* entry 184).

266.   Balachandran, Sarojini. **Employee Communication: A Bibliography**. An American Business Communication Association Publication. Urbana, IL: University of Illinois at Urbana-Champaign Library, 1976. 55 p.

A single list by author or title covers books, journals, and dissertations published between 1965 and 1975. Some entries have short annotations. Includes articles from *Public Relations Journal* and some of the basic communication journals. Useful for researching topics such as communication in management and employee publications, but lack of subject indexing results in tedious searching.

267.   Bishop, Robert L., comp. **Public Relations: A Comprehensive Bibliography; Articles and Books on Public Relations, Communication Theory, Public Opinion, and Propaganda, 1964-1972**. Ann Arbor, MI: University of Michigan Press, 1974. 212 p.

Continuing the two editions of Cutlip (1957 and 1965), Bishop includes approximately four thousand citations in some one hundred seventy subject categories. Includes an author index and special sections on bibliographies, indexes, and organizations. High relevance.

268.   Constantine, Karen K. **An Annotated and Extended Bibliography of Higher Education Marketing**. AMA Bibliography Series. Chicago: American Marketing Association, 1986. 71 p.

This bibliography is limited to articles published since 1980. Some annotations are taken from ERIC; others are original. Item arrangement is alphabetical with subject codes attached to individual entries. Low to moderate relevance for public relations.

269.   Dannelley, Paul. **Fund Raising and Public Relations: A Critical Guide to Literature and Resources**. Norman, OK: University of Oklahoma Press, 1986. 145 p.

Includes books, articles, associations, and periodicals from 1975 to 1985 with descriptive annotations. High relevance.

270.   Georgi, Charlotte, and Fate, Terry. **Fund-Raising, Grants and Foundations: A Comprehensive Bibliography**. Littleton, CO: Libraries Unlimited, 1985. 194 p.

A comprehensive list of fifteen hundred titles (books, pamphlets, and annuals) published since 1970. Arrangement is in three sections: reference sources, subject information resources (in ten categories), and a core-collection list (by publisher). High relevance.

271.   Gitter, A. George, and Grunin, Robert. **Communication: A Guide to Information Sources**. Detroit, MI: Gale, 1980. 157 p.

A selective bibliography, with brief annotations, of books and journal articles, most of which were published during the 1970s. Intended as a guide to the mainstream literature of the period in broad areas such as interpersonal, international, and political communication. However, most of the references are on the topic of mass communications. Low to moderate relevance.

272.   Greenbaum, Howard H.; Falcione, Raymond L.; and Hellweg, Susan A. **Organizational Communication: Abstracts, Analysis and Overview**. Newbury Park, CA: Sage, 1978- . (Annual)

Published in cooperation with the American Business Communication Association (now called Association for Business Communication) and the International Communication Association, this annual work consists of a survey and overview of recent literature, abstracts in a classified arrangement with annotations, and a review essay. Relevant for several areas of public relations interest, including analysis of communication systems and media.

273.   Kaid, Lynda L., and Wadsworth, Anne J. **Political Campaign Communication: A Bibliography and Guide to the Literature, 1973-1982**. Metuchen, NJ: Scarecrow, 1985. 217 p.

This work includes 2,461 unannotated entries (books and articles) in a single alphabetical arrangement with a keyword index. It was preceded by a 1974 edition that included a section entitled "Guide to the Literature," dropped from this edition. Relevant for political public relations topics.

274.   Larson, Keith A., comp. **Public Relations, the Edward L. Bernayses and the American Scene**. 2d ed. Boston: Faxon, 1978. 774 p.

A bibliography of writings by and about Bernays, covering the period from 1905 to 1977. This second edition extends the coverage of the original 1951 volume. Bernays is a prolific writer and speaker on the development and practice of public relations in this century. (Not examined.)

275.   Miles, William. **The Image Makers: A Bibliography of American Presidential Campaign Biographies**. Metuchen, NJ: Scarecrow, 1979. 254 p.

This work lists biographies of presidential candidates published during campaign periods from 1824 to 1976. Campaign biographies attempt to promote candidates through image building, and by emphasizing their presidential qualities, so this material might be relevant in the historical study of political public relations.

276.   Newman, Bruce I., and Sheth, Jagdish N., eds. **Political Marketing: Readings and an Annotated Bibliography**. Chicago: American Marketing Association, 1985. 259 p.

The editors include a seventy-page bibliography of books (published since the 1940s) and articles (most published in the mid-1980s) on such topics as candidate image building, effects of information on voters, and campaign strategy, including advertising and promotional tactics. Some material relevant to political public relations.

277. Norton, Alice. **Public Relations: Information Sources**. Management Information Guide 22. Detroit, MI: Gale, 1970. 153 p.

This work is organized in six sections: general sources, special fields and publics, public relations tools, associations, careers in public relations, and international aspects. Author, title, and subject indexes are provided. The annotations are descriptive and sometimes evaluative. This is the most useful bibliography for material on practical public relations up to 1970.

278. Public Relations Society of America. **Bibliography for Public Relations Professionals**. New York: PRSA. (Annual; twenty pages in the 1986 edition.)

A selective and unannotated list of recent books grouped under approximately forty subject headings. Includes directories and periodicals. The 1986 edition includes some four hundred entries. Intended for practitioners and for building professional libraries, with prices given for all items. High relevance as a selective guide to current literature.

279. Ryans, Cynthia C., and Shanklin, William L. **Strategic Planning, Marketing and Public Relations, and Fund-Raising in Higher Education: Perspectives, Readings, and Annotated Bibliography**. Metuchen, NJ: Scarecrow, 1986. 266 p.

Each section comprises an overview, readings, and a bibliography, combining practical advice with guidance for further study. The marketing and public relations section is relevant for public relations research. Books (most published since 1980) and periodicals are listed separately. Good relevance within its limited scope.

280. Shearer, Benjamin F., and Huxford, Marilyn, comps. **Communications and Society: A Bibliography on Communications Techniques and Their Social Impact**. Westport, CT: Greenwood, 1983. 242 p.

A collection of references on mass-media topics, including politics and advertising and the media. Useful for background material; covers books and journal articles over a period of approximately forty years.

281. **Vance Bibliographies**. Public Administration Series. Monticello, IL: Vance. (Irregular)

A series of short bibliographic lists on a wide range of topics not strictly limited to public administration. Recent titles relevant to public relations include *Police-Community Relations* (no. 2138, 29 p.), *The Corporate Image* (no. 1875, 9 p.), and *Lobbying* (no. 1068, 28 p.). List of titles is available from the publisher at P.O. Box 229, 112 N. Charter St., Monticello, IL 61856.

282. Walker, Albert, comp. **Public Relations Bibliography**. New York: Institute for Public Relations Research and Education. (Annual 1977 through 1986, Winter editions of **Public Relations Review**; biennial 1987- from IPRRE.)

This comprehensive annual bibliography is the current continuation of the bibliography initiated by Cutlip in the 1950s and 1960s and continued by Bishop in the mid-1970s (*see* entry 267). (The 1973-74 edition appeared as a supplement to the Winter 1976 issue of *Public Relations Review*; the 1975 edition appeared in the Summer 1977 issue.) Books, articles, and unpublished theses from the preceding year are included. The format and use of subject headings have varied over time, and books have been listed separately in some but not all editions. Cumbersome and scattered with typographical errors, but a thorough annual review of current literature and issues for public relations practitioners and researchers. Sponsored by the Institute for Public Relations Research and Education.

283. Weiner, Richard. **Professional's Guide to Public Relations Services**. 5th ed. New York: Public Relations Publishing, 1985. 532 p.

A practical listing of "over 2000 products, companies, services and techniques," including media directories, research services, periodicals and newsletters, and associations. The annotations are detailed and informal, reflecting the author's experience and personal opinions. High relevance for practical public relations activity. (Sixth edition, published by Amacom in 1988, not examined.)

284. Wyckham, Robert G.; Lazer, William; and Crissy, W. J. E., comps. **Images and Marketing: A Selected and Annotated Bibliography**. AMA Bibliography Series, no. 17. Chicago: American Marketing Association, 1971. 58 p.

The 244 entries are largely journal articles, with some books and reports of research. The material is organized in three parts: general concepts, measurement techniques, and empirical findings. Some entries relate to public relations.

INDEXES

Indexes are key research tools because they offer direct access to individual articles in magazines, journals, newspapers, and other sources in which the specific contents vary from one issue to another. In these sources, topics that are too narrow, specialized, or recent to appear in books may be treated; current developments in the field may be reported; and personal commentaries may be presented. Therefore, the literature of public relations is not fully revealed unless one examines the wide range of material that appears in the journals and periodicals.

The indexes to books, journal and periodical articles, and theses and dissertations described here provide access to the literature, both scholarly and popular, in communications and journalism, political science, business, and related fields. Some of these indexes are basic tools for both public and academic libraries; other, more specialized titles may not be generally available but will be found with substantial collections of related material.

In researching a public relations topic, the nature of the topic—whether it is mainly related to the communication, business, or political aspects of public relations—determines the indexes to be employed. Because the subject of public relations incorporates these different facets, an index that proves useful for one topic may be less relevant for other topics.

Several of the indexes listed here have identical or very similar counterparts in machine-readable form accessible through online searching services such as DIALOG and BRS. Many online databases perform the same function that printed indexes perform, but with enhancements. The listing of these index-like tools follows immediately after this section.

285. **Arts and Humanities Citation Index**. Philadelphia, PA: Institute for Scientific Information, 1976- . (Three issues per year, cumulated annually and every five years.)

This index, which allows searching by subject or cited author and which identifies review articles with many references, is a companion to *Social Sciences Citation Index* (entry 300). The major communication and journalism publications are indexed in both works. Available in online version (entry 305).

286. **Bibliographic Index**. New York: H. W. Wilson, 1938- . (Three issues per year, annual cumulations.)

Because this index includes not only separately published bibliographies but also any monograph or journal article with a substantial list of references, it is a useful tool for scanning the current literature. In recent years it has indexed material on public relations for hospitals, police officers, schools, libraries, athletic programs, and professional services. Available in online version (*see* entry 306).

287. **Business Index**. Belmont, CA: Information Access Company, 1979- . (Monthly; latest three years on microfilm with earlier years on microfiche.)

This index covers the major public relations and business journals, national newspapers, and regional business publications. Access is mainly by subject. A useful resource for locating recent material on practical public relations and corporate topics.

288. **Business Periodicals Index**. New York: H. W. Wilson, 1958- . (Monthly, annual cumulations.)

This very useful index offers subject access to the major public relations journals and many business and management publications; it also indexes book reviews by author. It is an important resource for locating information on general and corporate public relations, both theoretical and practical aspects. Subject headings to be found are public relations, public relations and politics, public relations ethics, public relations research, and many other relevant headings on corporate and political topics. Available in online and CD-ROM versions (entry 307).

289. **Communication Abstracts**. Newbury Park, CA: Sage, 1978- . (Quarterly)

This index, prepared at the Temple University School of Communications and Theater, includes approximately one thousand citations per year for books, book chapters, and journal articles in the areas of business, marketing, political science, journalism, sociology, psychology, education, media, speech communication, and general social science. A valuable resource in communications, providing access to some journals that are not indexed elsewhere. The entries in each issue are indexed by author and subject; index terms include public relations, political advertising, political communication, business communication, and government credibility. Most items are cited within two years of their publication. Many articles and subject headings relevant to public relations.

290. **Current Index to Journals in Education (CIJE)**. Phoenix, AZ: Oryx, 1969- . (Monthly, semiannual cumulations.)

This comprehensive index to educational journals also covers the major communications periodicals and *Public Relations Review*. A related index, *Resources in Education (RIE)*, covers the research literature not published in periodicals but available on microfiche from ERIC. Available in online and CD-ROM versions (*see* entry 310).

291. **Doctoral Dissertations in Political Science in Universities of the United States**. Washington, DC: American Political Science Association, 1911- . (Annual)

This list is arranged in two sections: dissertations in preparation and dissertations completed during the year. Since 1968, published in the Fall issue of the APSA's *PS: Newsletter of the American Political Science Association*.

292. **Educators Guide to Free Audio and Video Materials**. Randolph, WI: Educators Progress Service, Inc. (Annual)

This is one in a series of titles available from this publisher. Other titles in the series include *Educators Guide to Free Films* and *Educators Guide to Free Filmstrips and Slides*. The series provides access to the extensive body of materials produced for use in the schools to serve the goals of economic education and public relations. Media producers and distributors that specialize in sponsored films, such as Modern Talking Picture Service and West Glen Films, are included as are government, military, and state agencies; embassies; trade and service associations; and corporations.

293. **Humanities Index**. New York: H. W. Wilson, 1965- . (Quarterly, annual cumulations.)

This index includes journalism literature and thus contains references to public relations topics. However, it is not an essential tool for public relations research because the journalism periodicals are indexed more completely in other sources. Subject headings include public relations, corporate public relations, public service television, press agents, press conferences, and press releases. Available in online and CD-ROM versions (*see* entry 312).

294. **Journal of Business**. Chicago: University of Chicago Graduate School of Business. (Quarterly since 1956.)

Each year, the January issue of this journal lists doctoral dissertations accepted at American schools of business and management. Typical subject groupings include marketing, management and organization theory and practice, and public and nonprofit institutions.

295. **Journalism Abstracts**. Columbia, SC: Association for Education in Journalism and Mass Communication, 1963- . (Annual)

An index to doctoral dissertations and masters' theses in journalism and mass communications that were accepted at American universities during the previous year. Annual number of entries ranges from two hundred to almost four hundred, with up to fifty institutions represented. The abstracts are substantive and are prepared by the authors. Author, subject, and institution indexes are provided.

296. **JQ: Journalism Quarterly**. Columbia, SC: Association for Education in Journalism and Mass Communication. (Quarterly since 1924.)

This is an international index to articles on mass communications. Entries are arranged by subject, with public relations as one of the subject categories. Book reviews are included, also arranged by subject. Author and detailed topical indexes are provided annually. This is an important research resource with many items relevant to public relations. Cumulated in *Index to Journals* (entry 297) to 1985.

297. Matlon, Ronald J., and Facciola, Peter C., eds. **Index to Journals in Communication Studies Through 1985**. Annandale, VA: Speech Communication Association, 1987. 645 p.

This index covers fifteen major journals in speech, journalism, and communication from their beginnings to 1985. The editors use a coded system of subject classification, which makes the index rather difficult for the novice to use. However, the index provides access to many articles in the field of communication that are relevant to public relations.

298. NICEM Indexes. Los Angeles: National Information Center for Educational Media (at University of Southern California), 1969- .

A series of indexes to educational media in various formats and on a variety of subjects. Currently, there appears to be fourteen volumes in the set, each with a different publication date and updating schedule. Titles include *Educational Audio Tapes, Educational Videotapes, 35mm Educational Filmstrips, 8mm Motion Cartridges*, and *16mm Educational Films*. Subject volumes cover vocational and technical education, environmental studies, and Black studies. Available in online version as A-V Online (entry 301).

299. Public Affairs Information Service Bulletin (P.A.I.S.). New York: Public Affairs Information Service, 1915- . (Six issues per year, annual cumulations.)

This index provides access to a wide range of social-science and mass-media publications, including *Public Relations Review*. Its public affairs scope extends from international affairs to the local community, with extensive coverage of national and urban political and public administration topics and the mass media. Access is provided by subject only. Library of Congress subject headings are used; they include campaigns, communication in politics, government information, lobbying, political consultants, and political action committees. Available in online and CD-ROM versions (*see* entry 314).

300. Social Sciences Citation Index. Philadelphia, PA: Institute for Scientific Information, 1972- . (Three issues per year, cumulated annually and every five years.)

This index to the major journals in communication and political science also covers *Public Relations Review*. The permuted term subject index, a special feature of this publication, includes many citations to public relations articles. Companion index to *Arts and Humanities Citation Index* (entry 285). Available in online version as Social Scisearch (entry 319).

301. Social Sciences Index. New York: H. W. Wilson, 1965- . (Quarterly, annual cumulations.)

Political science and public administration articles are indexed here, as are communication and business periodicals. Provides access to material on public relations in particular types of organizations and on public communication topics. Subject headings include business and politics, business-social aspects, corporate image, government publicity, and public relations as a subheading under various types of officials and institutions. Available in online and CD-ROM versions (*see* entry 318).

302. United States Political Science Documents. Pittsburgh, PA: NASA Industrial Applications Center, 1975- . (Annual)

This source indexes and provides abstracts for articles from a wide range of political-science journals. Subjects include political communication, influence process, election-campaign tactics, communication analysis, and media studies.

ONLINE RESOURCES

A number of online databases contain information about public relations theory and practice. Some of them have print counterparts, which have been included in the list of indexes. Online databases, however, provide information and service in a way not possible in print, either because they provide new ways of accessing the material (for example, any combination of terms from article titles or abstracts) or because they index publications not previously accessible (for example, those covered by the PR newsline services). The online services industry and related technologies, such as compact disks (noted in the listings as CD-ROM products), are presently in a growth stage, so new services and databases not noted here will probably be available by the time this work is published. A monthly newspaper of the information industry, *Information Today*, is a useful source on new products in this field.

The online databases included here are widely available in academic and public libraries. Most of them are also directly accessible to researchers through the major online service vendors, DIALOG and BRS. The Wilsonline databases produced by H. W. Wilson are available by arrangement with that company.

Dates in the online citations here refer to their current scope of content (coverage), not to the dates the services became available.

303. **ABI/Inform**. Ann Arbor, MI: University Microfilms, 1971- .
One of the basic databases for searching the business literature, including among its indexed titles the major English-language journals in business, management, and public relations (including British and Canadian publications). From 1971 to 1987, over sixty-eight hundred articles in the database were indexed under the term *public relations*. Highly relevant for business-government relations, corporate image, and other topics in corporate public relations. Also available as a CD-ROM product.

304. **A-V Online**. Albuquerque, NM: Access Innovations.
Online counterpart of the print series NICEM Indexes (entry 298). Access to this database of educational media is provided by descriptive terms, subject codes, producers and distributors, media type, grade level, and more. Includes relevant entries under the terms *public relations* and *economic education.*

305. **Arts and Humanities Search**. Philadelphia, PA: Institute for Scientific Information, 1980- .
Online version of *Arts and Humanities Subject Citation Index* (entry 285).

306. **Bibliographic Index**. Bronx, NY: Wilsonline, November 1984- .
Online version of the print index of the same name (entry 286).

307. **Business Periodicals Index**. Bronx, NY: Wilsonline, June 1982- .
Online version of the print index of the same name (entry 288). Also available on CD-ROM. Wilson also produces CD-ROM versions of *Humanities Index* (entry 293) and *Social Sciences Index* (entry 301).

308. **BusinessWire**. San Francisco, CA: Business Wire, 1986- .
This database consists of the full text of news releases generated by corporations and other organizations. Therefore, it represents the products of public relations workers. The content is updated daily and may be searched by words in the text, news-release titles, company names, dateline, or publication date.

309. **Dissertation Abstracts Online**. Ann Arbor, MI: University Microfilms, 1861- .
An index to American doctoral dissertations and some master's theses in all academic fields. A print version is also available, but the expanded searching capability of the online version makes it considerably more useful than its print counterpart. Also available as a CD-ROM product.

310. **ERIC**. Washington, DC: U.S. Department of Education, Educational Resources Information Center, 1966- (documents) and 1969- (journal coverage).

This source, combining *CIJE* (entry 290) and *RIE* in an online format, is the core database for educational literature. It includes reports on educational public relations and advancement as well as material on public relations curricula in higher education. Indexes journals (including *Public Relations Review*) and other documents, including papers from meetings of the Association for Education in Journalism and Mass Communication. Also available as a CD-ROM product.

311. **Harvard Business Review**. New York: Wiley, 1971- .

An online index to the print journal, including, since 1976, the full text of articles.

312. **Humanities Index**. Bronx, NY: Wilsonline, 1984- .

Online version of entry 293. Also available as a CD-ROM product.

313. **Management Contents**. Belmont, CA: Information Access Company, 1974- .

With ABI/Inform (entry 303), this is a core database for business and management literature. Like ABI/Inform, it indexes the major public relations journals and a wide selection of management journals.

314. **P.A.I.S. International**. New York: Public Affairs Information Service, 1976- .

Online counterpart of the print index *Public Affairs Information Service Bulletin (P.A.I.S.)* (entry 299) plus the contents of the *P.A.I.S. Foreign Language Index* (1972-). Also available as a CD-ROM product.

315. **PRLink**. New York: PRSA. (Current)

A database of current public relations news and information and a job bulletin board. Also provides an electronic mail service and opportunities to participate in online forum discussions. For public relations professionals by subscription through CompuServe.

316. **PR Newswire**. New York: PR Newswire Association, Inc., May 1987- .

Another database with the full text of news releases, including more records than BusinessWire (entry 308), with reports from companies, trade associations, public relations consultants, and government agencies. The contents are heavily weighted toward business and financial news and are updated every fifteen minutes.

317. **PsycINFO**. Arlington, VA: American Psychological Association, 1967- .

Most of the public relations articles indexed here are related to social and health services. Other related topics with psychological content, such as persuasion and interpersonal communication, can be searched in this database. Also available in CD-ROM as PsycLIT.

318. **Social Sciences Index**. Bronx, NY: Wilsonline, 1983- .

Online version of *Social Sciences Index* (entry 301). Also available as a CD-ROM product.

319. **Social Scisearch**. Philadelphia, PA: Institute for Scientific Information, 1972- .

Online counterpart to *Social Sciences Citation Index* (entry 300).

320. **Sociological Abstracts**. San Diego, CA: Sociological Abstracts, Inc., 1963- .

Also includes a subfile, "Social Planning/Policy and Development Abstracts," that indexes applied social research.

321. **Trade and Industry Index**. Belmont, CA: Information Access Company, 1981- .
Valuable for its coverage of national and regional newspapers and a wide range of trade publications.

PUBLISHERS AND SPONSORS OF SERIES

322. **American Management Association**. 135 W. 50th St., New York, NY 10020.
Since 1923, this organization has provided programs, products, and services to meet the continuing-education needs of managers. It publishes several major business journals, including *Management Review, Management Solutions*, and *Personnel*, and under the Amacom imprint many books on corporate and nonprofit management topics. *See* entries 89, 91, 283, 348, 354, 356, 360, 361, 366, 376, 377, 387, 394, 411, 447, 469, and 589.

323. **Columbia University, Graduate School of Business**. Uris Hall, New York, NY 10027. Richard Eells, program director.
Studies of the Modern Corporation, a series designed to advance and disseminate knowledge about the modern corporation, includes works by outstanding businessmen and scholars, annotated and edited selections from the business literature, and reprinted classics. *See* entries 426, 434, 435, and 439.

324. **Conference Board**. 845 Third Ave., New York, NY 10022.
The Conference Board, a major producer of studies and surveys for business executives in American, Canadian, and European corporations, prepares an annual index to its full range of publications. Among the index subject categories are public relations, investor relations, government-industry relations, social responsibility, urban affairs, political affairs, and public affairs. The Conference Board Report series includes many relevant titles cited throughout this bibliography. A Research Bulletin series includes shorter surveys and reports. *See* entries 248, 344, 345, 363, 378, 383, 384, 386, 390, 401, 404, 405, 422, 425, 428, 431, 432, 433, 453, 459, 460, 461, and 466.

325. **Investor Responsibility Research Center**. 1755 Massachusetts Ave. N.W., Suite 600, Washington, DC 20038.
This organization publishes reports on and analyses of social issues and public policies that affect corporations and their investors. *See also News for Investors* (entry 258), and *Proxy Issues Report* (entry 259).

326. **Longman, Inc.** 95 Church St., White Plains, NY 10601.
Longman Series in Public Communication, edited by Ray E. Hiebert. Titles include *Experts in Action* (entry 6); *Informing the Public* (entry 481); *On Deadline* (entry 114); *Longman Dictionary of Mass Media and Communication* (entry 88); *Public Relations Management by Objectives* (entry 125); *Inside Organizational Communications* (entry 369); *Raising the Bottom Line* (entry 445); and *Community Relations Handbook* (entry 593).

4

Corporate Public Relations

Corporate public relations creates and monitors the communication links that build goodwill between the corporation and its internal and external publics. (Generally excepted from the public relations function are those communications relating strictly to products and personnel management.) The publics with which corporations are involved include customers, competitors, suppliers, employers, shareholders, the financial community, the public media, the immediate community, government entities at all levels, legislators, academia, minority groups, conservationists and other special interest groups, the church, and the general public. The development of new communications technologies, increasing international competition, and the growth of social pressures on the corporation have all contributed to changes in the practice of corporate public relations in the second half of this century.

To assist users looking for additional or more recent material, this and the following two chapters provide standard Library of Congress subject headings for topics for which the search terms are not self-evident. This information is included in recognition of the fact that not all library collections are accessible through online catalogs that can respond to an unlimited subject vocabulary.

In this chapter, four particular aspects of corporate public relations are treated first: image building (including corporate-identity planning), economic education, advocacy advertising, and issues management. The first two activities are traditional public relations concerns; the last two have emerged over the past twenty years largely in response to increased pressures from society and government.

IMAGE BUILDING

Effective image building programs seek to create favorable corporate images through every form of public encounter, from a carefully structured advertising program to the most casual gossip and rumor. Much effort is expended not only on image building in the media but also in devising appropriate visual symbols through corporate graphics, building architecture, and office design. However, a corporation's image is largely shaped by its actions, and the manner in which it responds to external pressures, particularly to crises, has a powerful effect on its public image. Examples frequently cited include Johnson & Johnson's handling of the Tylenol scare and Union Carbide's response to the Bhopal disaster.

In library collections that use Library of Congress cataloging, information on this topic appears under the subject heading Corporate image.

327.   Garbett, Thomas F. **Corporate Advertising: The What, the Why and the How**. New York: McGraw-Hill, 1981. 252 p.

This work describes various types of nonproduct corporate advertising—image building, public service ads, and constituency advertising—excluding advocacy advertising. The author provides practical guidance with many illustrations and examples. Also by this author: *How to Build a Corporation's Identity and Project Its Image* (Lexington, MA: Lexington, 1988. Not examined.)

328.   Gray, James G., Jr. **Managing the Corporate Image: The Key to Public Trust**. Westport, CT: Quorum, 1986. 164 p. notes.

Written for corporate public relations managers, this book includes case studies and guidelines for measuring the impact of an image-building program.

329.   Koenig, Fredrick. **Rumor in the Marketplace: The Social Psychology of Commercial Hearsay**. Dover, MA: Auburn, 1985. 180 p. notes.

A general study of commercial rumors and their control, written by a social psychologist. Particularly relevant for the study of corporate crisis management.

Corporate Identity

Corporate identity, an aspect of corporate image building, here refers to the tangible aspects, especially the visual elements, of the corporate image.

330.   Carter, David E. **Designing Corporate Identity Programs for Small Corporations**. New York: Art Direction, 1982. 333 p.

Intended for designers and design students, small business executives, and communications and marketing officers, this book provides guidance on developing corporate identity. The greater part of its content consists of case studies from a variety of settings, including institutions.

331.   Graphic Artists Guild. **Graphic Artists Guild's Corporate and Communications Design Annual**. New York: Annuals Publishing. (Annual)

This brief volume consists of examples of corporate graphics, most in color, indexed by artist and client. Of interest mainly to art students, designers, and advertising agencies. (1984 volume examined.)

332.   Napoles, Veronica. **Corporate Identity Design**. New York: Van Nostrand Reinhold, 1988. 144 p.

A practical guide to developing a corporate image that represents the corporate identity. Reviewed in *Public Relations Review* (Summer 1988). (Not examined.)

333.   Olins, Wally. **The Corporate Personality: An Inquiry into the Nature of Corporate Identity**. London: Design Council, 1978. 215 p.

A general introduction, for executives and students, to corporate identity and how it is controlled through visual symbols. Contemporary and historical examples are included, mostly from Great Britain. The author is a British design consultant.

334. Olins, Wally. **The Wolff Olins Guide to Corporate Identity**. London: Wolff Olins, 1984. 56 p. bibliography.

A greatly abbreviated version of the preceding work, this guide to the visual projection of corporate identity also includes numerous examples from the United States and Western Europe.

See also Selame and Selame, *Developing a Corporate Identity* (entry 136), and a more recent title by the same authors, *The Company Image: Building Your Identity and Influence in the Marketplace* (New York: Wiley, 1988; 230 p.).

ECONOMIC EDUCATION

Traditionally, corporate economic-education programs have been directed toward public education and the corporation's own shareholders and employees. More recently, corporations have used advocacy advertising in the mass media to attempt to education the public on economic issues. That division has been retained here; this section deals with economic education in the traditional sense; the following section deals with advocacy advertising.

335. Budd, John F., Jr. **Corporate Video in Focus: A Management Guide to Private TV**. Englewood Cliffs, NJ: Prentice-Hall, 1983. 210 p. notes.

A practical and promotional guide to the use of cable television for corporate educational communications, annual reports, news releases, corporate magazine-type material, and conferencing. The author is a public relations executive.

336. Emanuel, Myron, et al. **Corporate Economic Education Programs: An Evaluation and Appraisal**. New York: Financial Executives Research Foundation, 1979. 382 p.

A review of print and nonprint business programs developed for schools, employees, shareholders, and the general public, with identification of common pitfalls of such programs. The authors' approach to program evaluation is still relevant, even though some of the program examples are now out of date.

337. Harty, Sheila. **Hucksters in the Classroom: A Review of Industry Propaganda in Schools**. Washington, DC: Center for Study of Responsive Law, 1979. 190 p. notes. bibliography.

A critical examination of corporate educational media, including examples of educational program evaluations programs, the role of the Federal Trade Commission, industry self-regulation, and citizen initiatives. Special coverage with examples is provided for material on nutrition, energy, the environment, and economics.

See also Educators Guide to Free Audio and Video Materials (entry 292).

ADVOCACY ADVERTISING

Advocacy advertising, also called issue advertising, is a fairly recent development. An early and certainly the best-known advocacy advertising campaign was that of the Mobil Corporation in 1974 during the oil crisis. Advocacy ads present, in print or audiovisual media, a point of view on a social or economic topic; the message is not clearly linked to a particular company, although the sponsor is required to identify itself somewhere in the ad. Controversy advertising, defined by Stridsberg (entry 341) as advertising that presents information or a point of view on a controversial public issue, is also included here. Advocacy and controversy advertising represent a new form of economic education, with the general public, thought leaders, and other corporate managers as the intended targets. One area of particular interest for advocacy advertising is the question of whether the media have an obligation to accept this type of advertising. In the past, the Fairness Doctrine has been used by television networks to limit the amount of advocacy advertising accepted. This doctrine requires that all sides of controversial public issues be given balanced public airing, a constraint that the networks have tried to avoid by refusing to present controversial issues at all.

338.   Schmertz, Herbert. **Good-bye to the Low Profile: The Art of Creative Confrontation**. Boston: Little, Brown, 1986. 242 p.

The author, vice-president for public affairs at Mobil Corporation, describes his company's well-publicized program for confronting issues in the public media and in relations with government agencies.

339.   Sethi, S. Prakash. **Advocacy Advertising and Large Corporations: Social Conflict, Big Business Image, the News Media, and Public Policy**. Lexington, MA: Heath, 1977. 355 p. notes. bibliography.

The scope of advocacy advertising, its benefits to corporations, and legal aspects are covered. The author advocates corporate social responsibility. Includes case studies, examples of ads, and an extensive bibliography.

340.   Sethi, S. Prakash. **Handbook of Advocacy Advertising: Concepts, Strategies, and Applications**. Cambridge, MA: Ballinger, 1987. 577 p. notes.

A substantial part of this illustrated book presents case studies from corporations, associations, state-owned entities, and unions.

341.   Stridsberg, Albert B. **Controversy Advertising: How Advertisers Present Points of View in Public Affairs**. New York: Hastings (sponsored by the International Advertising Association), 1977. 189 p.

Controversy advertising is defined as advertising that presents information or a point of view on a controversial public issue. A study of origin, development, and current practice in twenty-four countries. The focus is mainly corporate, but government-sponsored advertising is also considered. Thirty-two cases from the United States, Europe, and the Third World are included.

342.   Warner, Rawleigh, Jr., and Silk, Leonard. **Ideals in Collision: The Relationship between Business and the News Media**. Benjamin F. Fairless Memorial Lectures, 1978. Pittsburgh, PA: Carnegie-Mellon University Press, 1979. 63 p.

Essays by two authors. Warner's essay on Mobil Corporation's advocacy-advertising program is most relevant to corporate public relations.

ISSUES MANAGEMENT

Issues management comprises a group of corporate activities: monitoring the environments of business to anticipate emerging issues that will have an impact on the corporation, selecting and analyzing priority issues, developing strategy options, and implementing planned actions. Crisis management is one aspect of this public relations function. To be effective, issues management must be a part of the corporation's public policy process, which is a top management function. The nature and quality of formal and informal communication between the public relations office and top management is therefore a topic of particular concern in issues management. In 1982, the Issue Management Association was established to encourage communication among executives with responsibility for issues management.

Subject headings under which this topic may be indexed in library catalogs include Crisis management, Issues management, and Corporations, U.S.--Public opinion.

343. Andriole, Stephen J., ed. **Corporate Crisis Management**. Princeton, NJ: Petrocelli, 1985. 316 p. notes.

Contributions by academic, government, and private-sector policy analysts on the need for strategic planning and preparation for crises. Public relations is not an explicit topic in the discussion.

344. Brown, James K. **Guidelines for Managing Corporate Issues Programs**. Conference Board Report no. 795. New York: Conference Board, 1981. 35 p. notes.

Using examples from actual corporations, the author defines the corporate issues program and describes the monitoring process. This handbook-style work is a revision of report no. 758 (entry 345).

345. Brown, James K. **This Business of Issues: Coping with the Company's Environments**. Conference Board Report no. 758. New York: Conference Board, 1979. 74 p. notes.

The report of a survey on how corporations are monitoring and responding to public policy issues. The author describes various methods of classifying trends, environmental scanning, and action planning, and gives examples.

346. Chase, W. Howard. **Issue Management: Origins of the Future**. Stamford, CT: Issue Action Publications, 1984. 170 p. bibliography.

The author, a leader in issues management, describes his model and urges inclusion of the public relations function at the vice-presidential level for more effective policy management.

347. Ewing, Raymond P. **Managing the New Bottom Line: Issues Management for Senior Executives**. Homewood, IL: Dow Jones-Irwin, 1987. 191 p. notes.

The author discusses the development of an issues-management program, drawing on his experiences in establishing one for Allstate and as cofounder of the Issue Management Association. He defines issues management as a distinct form of corporate planning, similar but not identical to strategic planning.

348. Fink, Steven. **Crisis Management: Planning for the Inevitable**. New York: Amacom, 1986. 245 p.

Actual examples of corporate crises are used to support the author's appeal for a planned, proactive system of corporate crisis management.

349. Heath, Robert L., and Associates, eds. **Strategic Issues Management: How Organizations Influence and Respond to Public Interests and Policies**. San Francisco, CA: Jossey-Bass, 1988. 415 p. bibliography.

Heath, director of the Institute for the Study of Issues Management at the University of Houston, stresses the importance of knowledge of public issues for effective strategic planning. Contributors to this volume examine organizational tactics for issues management, corporate external communication, lobbying, political action committees (PACs), relationships with trade associations and other public information organizations, and the future of issues management.

350. Health, Robert L., and Nelson, Richard A. **Issues Management: Corporate Public Policymaking in an Information Society**. Newbury Park, CA: Sage, 1986. 288 p. bibliography.

The authors define issues management broadly as activities and attitudes designed to foster public understanding of the corporation and to facilitate the corporation's adjustment to its environment. This work surveys the development and present practice of corporate issues management and includes consideration of government regulation, campaign practices, the role of special-interest groups, and the impact of new technology. An extensive bibliography is included.

351. Johnson, M. Bruce, ed. **The Attack on Corporate America: The Corporate Issues Sourcebook**. New York: McGraw-Hill, 1978. 348 p. bibliography.

A selection of the most important issues faced by American corporations, with pro-and-con summaries on each issue based on economic arguments. Topics include social responsibility, employee relations, manager-owner conflict, market power, profits, and regulation.

352. Lerbinger, Otto. **Managing Corporate Crises: Strategies for Executives**. Boston: Barrington Press, 1986. 101 p. notes.

Examples of four types of crises—technological, confrontational, malevolent, and management failure—are presented, and appropriate communication responses are prescribed.

353. Lesly, Philip. **Overcoming Opposition: A Survival Manual for Executives**. Englewood Cliffs, NJ: Prentice-Hall, 1984. 212 p.

The author takes an adversarial view of confrontations between corporate management and public activists, and the latter groups tend to be stereotyped. Appropriate modes of persuasive communication for corporations are suggested.

354. Littlejohn, Robert F. **Crisis Management: A Team Approach**. AMA Management Briefing. New York: American Management Association, 1983. 54 p.

A short overview on organizing for effective response to corporate crises, early detection, and contingency planning.

355. Meyers, Gerald C. **When It Hits the Fan: Managing the Nine Crises of Business**. Boston: Houghton Mifflin, 1986. 271 p.

This book is written for corporate executives by a former executive. Its approach is pragmatic with many short case studies as examples. The nine types of crises are public perception, market shifts, product failure, a change in top management, cash shortages, industrial-relations problems, hostile takeovers, international events, and regulatory problems.

356. Newton, Charles G., Jr. **Coming to Grips with Crisis**. AMA Special Study no. 76. New York: American Management Association, 1981. 47 p.

A short overview on the topic of corporate crisis management.

357. Pinsdorf, Marion K. **Communicating When Your Company Is under Siege: Surviving Public Crisis**. Lexington, MA: Lexington, 1987. 171 p. notes. bibliography.

While the subject of the book is stated to be corporate communications, the functions described are those of public relations. The author criticizes public relations practitioners for being overly concerned with defining their mission instead of truly communicating.

358. Stanley, Guy D. **Managing External Issues: Theory and Practice**. Greenwich, CT: Jai Press, 1985. 259 p. bibliography.

The author proposes a rational approach to strategic planning using economic models as a means to effective issues management.

CONSUMER RELATIONS

The most recent wave of consumer activism, which began in the early 1960s, has made corporations aware of the importance of good consumer relations not just for profitable operation but for corporate survival. From their early function of receiving consumer complaints, the operations of consumer-relations departments have expanded to include such activities as managing proactive consumer programs, measuring corporate effectiveness in customer satisfaction, and even acting as consumer advocate before management.

Subject headings for researching this topic include Consumer affairs departments, Customer relations, and Customer service.

359. Best, Arthur. **When Consumers Complain**. New York: Columbia University Press, 1981. 232 p. notes.

Using results of a consumer survey and interviews, the author examines problems in the consumer-complaint process and suggests possible reforms. Though not on the subject of consumer relations, the study is useful background reading.

360. Birsner, E. Patricia, and Balsley, Ronald D. **Practical Guide to Consumer Service Management and Operations**. New York: Amacom, 1982. 216 p. bibliography.

The authors describe a variety of consumer-service roles, emphasizing the communication function. In addition to covering the basic management functions, they give special attention to managing conflict and problem solving.

361. Bohl, Don L., ed. **Close to the Customer: An American Management Association Research Report on Consumer Affairs**. Foreword by John Guaspari. New York: American Management Association Publications, 1987. 96 p.

A survey of consumer-affairs departments in large corporations indicates that the major methods for communicating with existing and potential customers are toll-free telephone numbers, focus groups, and surveys.

362. Fornell, Claes. **Consumer Input for Marketing Decisions: A Study of Corporate Departments for Consumer Affairs**. Praeger Special Studies in U.S. Economic, Social & Political Issues. New York: Praeger, 1976. 164 p. bibliography.

An academic study of the role of consumer affairs in large corporations, its influence on marketing decision making, and its place in the organizational structure.

363. McGuire, E. Patrick. **The Consumer Affairs Department: Organization and Functions**. Conference Board Report no. 609. New York: Conference Board, 1973. 114 p. bibliography.

Using examples from companies surveyed, the author groups the major functions of consumer-affairs departments into the categories of complaint handling, consumer information, and advisory communication to the industry and to other units of the corporation.

364. Meer, Claudia G. **Customer Education**. Chicago: Nelson-Hall, 1984. 159 p. bibliography.

A study of a single aspect of consumer relations, this work discusses small-group demonstrations, workshops, seminars, and courses of up to three weeks duration. Extensive case studies are used to illustrate the objectives, structure, costs, methods, and evaluation of corporate customer-education programs.

EMPLOYEE RELATIONS

The corporation's employees represent one of its critical internal publics. Their attitudes can have a significant positive or negative impact on the corporation's public image and its community and political relations. The subject of management-employee communication is a part of the broader subject, personnel management; it also is included in literature on organization communication and, to some extent, industrial relations. Employee-relations communicators are responsible for ensuring that employees have accurate and credible information about company policies and a sense of involvement in the organization; these goals may be implemented through print communication organs, such as employee magazines and newsletters; regular meetings between employees and management representatives; and programs for assessing employees' opinions and responding to their concerns.

Subject headings for this topic include Communication in management, Communication in organizations, and Communication in personnel management.

365. Brody, E. W. **Communicating for Survival: Coping with Diminishing Human Resources.** New York: Praeger, 1987. 264 p. bibliographies.

The author, an educator and public relations counselor, describes organizational communication tasks and appropriate qualifications for the work. He advocates educational preparation that includes courses in communication, economics, management, corporate planning, and the social sciences.

366. D'Aprix, Roger M. **The Believable Corporation.** New York: Amacom, 1977. 211 p. notes.

The importance of communication for productive employee relations is the subject of this book, which is based on the author's experience.

367. D'Aprix, Roger M. **Communicating for Productivity.** New York: Harper, 1982. 112 p.

A general work on the uses of communication in personnel management. The author uses fictitious cases to illustrate his points and, in a final section, provides answers to practical questions about employee communications.

368. Deutsch, Arnold. **The Human Resources Revolution: Communicate or Litigate.** New York: McGraw-Hill, 1979. 246 p.

Discussion of a corporate communications program for managing communications with both internal and external publics. The functions described are those of public relations, although the organizing concept here is human-resources communication.

369. Reuss, Carol, and Silvis, Donn E., eds. **Inside Organizational Communications.** Longman Series in Public Communication. White Plains, NY: Longman, 1981. 336 p. bibliography.

Sponsored by the International Association of Business Communicators, this volume includes contributions from academia and the corporate world on organizing for internal communication, media use, legal aspects, evaluation, and trends. A list of IABC Gold Quill Award winners is included.

370. Steele, Fritz, and Jenks, Stephen. **The Feel of the Work Place: Understanding and Improving Organizational Climate.** Reading, MA: Addison-Wesley, 1977. 194 p. bibliography.

Factors that affect the internal environment of the corporation, including communications, management styles, and the reward system; some aspects are relevant to employee-relations management.

See also Balachandran, *Employee Communication: A Bibliography* (entry 266).

INVESTOR AND FINANCIAL RELATIONS

The corporation's shareholders represent another critical internal public. Investors, however, are only one of the publics that concern the financial public relations specialist; in *Lesly's Public Relations Handbook* (entry 87), twelve publics are identified, including securities analysts and dealers, bankers, investment-advisory services, institutional investors, and representatives of the financial press. Because financial public relations requires specialized knowledge of disclosure regulations and corporate finance, this function is often handled separately from the other major public relations activities. The principal forms of communication involved are the corporation's annual report to shareholders and the annual meeting, financial news releases, and interviews and presentations in which company officials describe the company's financial position to the media or potential investors. A recent additional responsibility is to prepare and disseminate information to sensitize shareholders to the dangers of a takeover.

To find material on this subject, use the Library of Congress subject heading Corporations--Investor relations.

371. Graves, Joseph J., Jr. **Managing Investor Relations: Strategies and Techniques**. Homewood, IL: Dow Jones-Irwin, 1982. 373 p. notes.

This work provides thorough coverage of the corporate financial environment, with chapters on corporate advertising, meeting management, and merger-related strategy.

372. Hill & Knowlton. **The SEC, the Securities Markets, and Your Financial Communications: Disclosure and Filing Requirements for Public Companies**. 5th ed. New York: Hill & Knowlton, 1979. 127 p.

This expanded version of a work first published in 1967 provides basic information on legal requirements for corporate reporting. Earlier editions had a slightly different title. Now outdated.

373. Kirsch, Donald. **Financial and Economic Journalism: Analysis, Interpretation and Reporting**. New York: New York University Press, 1978. 343 p. notes.

A text for journalism students on financial reporting, this work is useful for its exposition of financial relations from the reporter's side.

374. Marcus, Bruce W. **Competing for Capital in the '80s: An Investor Relations Approach**. rev. ed. Westport, CT: Quorum, 1983. 305 p. bibliography.

Written for corporate executives, this book provides practical and detailed coverage of competitive investor-relations techniques and includes outlines of presentations and documents.

375. Nichols, Donald R., ed. **Handbook of Investor Relations**. Homewood, IL: Dow Jones-Irwin, 1988. 400 p.

Contributions by financial-relations specialists. (Not examined.)

376. Roalman, Arthur R. **Investor Relations That Work**. New York: Amacom, 1980. 277 p.

Most of this volume consists of examples of annual and other corporate reports.

377. Roalman, Arthur R., ed. **Investor Relations Handbook**. New York: Amacom, 1974. 234 p.

Sponsored by the National Investor Relations Institute, this volume covers financial-relations activity in American and European companies. It also includes two case histories and an extensive appendix with laws, policies, and sources of assistance.

PUBLIC AFFAIRS

Public affairs is frequently used to describe a corporate function that keeps top management in touch with the external environment. The corporate public affairs office often has responsibility for issues management; environmental scanning and public opinion monitoring; managing the corporation's relationships with the media, the immediate community, and all levels of government; and corporate giving programs. Less frequently, corporate public affairs offices handle financial relations, advertising and consumer affairs, corporate-identity graphics development, and customer relations. Among the tools used in public affairs management are lobbying, advocacy and public service advertising, and other forms of economic education.

Some additional subject headings that are useful for locating material on this topic include Business and politics and Industry--Social aspects.

378.   Brown, James K. and Lusterman, Seymour. **Business and the Development of Ghetto Enterprise**. Conference Board Report no. 517. New York: Conference Board, 1971. 105 p.

A descriptive report on a particular type of corporate assistance program, problems in its application, and community reactions.

379.   Gollner, Andrew B. **Social Change and Corporate Strategy: The Expanding Role of Public Affairs**. Stamford, CT: Issue Action Publications, 1983. 205 p. notes. bibliography.

The author views public relations as a component of public affairs, which is defined as the management of an organization's relations with its environment. He cites an inter-penetrating systems model in urging that the public affairs function become an integral part of corporate decision making. An extensive bibliography is included.

380.   Human Resources Network, comp. **The Handbook of Corporate Social Responsibility: Profiles of Involvement**. 2d ed. Radnor, PA: Chilton, 1975. 629 p.

Social-action programs of corporations, 743 in all, are described in this work. They are arranged in twenty-seven categories ("interest areas"), including the arts, education, the environment, and job training. The descriptions include information on the motivation for programs, measures of success, and cosponsors.

381.   Kruckeberg, Dean, and Starck, Kenneth. **Public Relations and Community: A Reconstructed Theory**. New York: Praeger, 1988. 142 p. notes. bibliography.

Starting from a specific definition of public relations as "the active attempt to restore and maintain a sense of community" (p. xi), the authors present a case study (Standard Oil Company of Indiana). Their thesis is based on a sociological theory of loss of community developed at the turn of the century by Dewey, Veblen, and others at the University of Chicago. An up-to-date, eight-page bibliography is included.

382.   Lamb, Robert; Armstrong, William G., Jr.; and Morigi, Karolyn R. **Business, Media and the Law: The Troubled Confluence**. New York: New York University Press, 1980. 137 p. notes. bibliography.

Business is exhorted to attend to its public relations and social responsibilities in this work, which examines the development of adversarial relationships among business, government, and the media.

383. Lusterman, Seymour. **Managerial Competence: The Public Affairs Aspects.** Conference Board Report no. 805. New York: Conference Board, 1981. 42 p. notes. bibliography.

Analyzing a survey of corporations, the author calls for improvement in executive skills and leadership in public affairs to meet increasing external pressures.

384. Lusterman, Seymour. **Organization and Staffing of Corporate Public Affairs.** Conference Board Report no. 894. New York: Conference Board, 1987. 31 p.

Analysis of a survey indicating areas and levels of corporate public affairs responsibility.

385. Mahon, John F. **The Corporate Public Affairs Office: Structure, Behavior and Impact.** DBA thesis, Graduate School of Management, Boston University. Ann Arbor, MI: University Microfilms, 1982. 521 p. bibliography.

An examintion of the development of the corporate public affairs department and its effects on corporate behavior. Includes a detailed study of the chemical industry and Superfund legislation. Extensive bibliography.

386. McGrath, Phyllis S. **Managing Corporate External Relations: Changing Perspectives and Responses.** Conference Board Report no. 679. New York: Conference Board, 1976. 83 p.

One of the Conference Board's numerous reports on corporate public affairs. Two subsequent reports, *Business Credibility: The Critical Factors* (Report no. 701), and *Action Plans for Public Affairs* (Report no. 733), give the views of corporate executives on appropriate corporate actions and describe several cases of effective response.

387. Nagelschmidt, Joseph S., ed. **Public Affairs Handbook.** New York: Amacom in association with Fraser/Associates, Washington, DC, 1982. 301 p. notes.

Essays by corporate executives, public affairs managers, and educators, with a focus on practical aspects of public affairs management. The scope is broader than the title suggests, as all corporate publics are viewed as being affected by public policy.

388. Ross, Robert D. **The Management of Public Relations: Analysis and Planning External Relations.** New York: Wiley, 1977. 274 p. notes.

Written for corporate managers, this work describes how to successfully manage the corporation's relations with its publics. Specific areas of activity that are discussed include public affairs, community relations, corporate contributions, and financial relations.

389. Steckmest, Francis W. **Corporate Performance: The Key to Public Trust.** New York: McGraw-Hill, 1982. 295 p. notes.

Based on a Business Roundtable Resource and Review Committee study, this work describes fifteen major public and corporate governance issues that corporate managers need to address and recommends ways for corporations to improve responsiveness to the social environment.

390. Troy, Kathryn. **Studying and Addressing Community Needs: A Corporate Case Book.** Conference Board Report no. 866. New York: Conference Board, 1985. 46 p.

The development and application of a community-needs assessment program is described, with examples and action plans.

MEDIA RELATIONS

From the corporate perspective, media relations encompasses the representation of the corporation in newspapers, magazines, radio, and television; in news reports, regular columns, editorials and special features; and through interviews and press coverage of corporate events. Preparation and distribution of material for dissemination through the mass media is a major public relations activity.

Media relations may well be the most demanding aspect of public relations work, for the press has been the source of much of the negative "PR" regarding the practice of public relations. On the corporate side, the aspect of media relations that receives considerable attention is the bad press accorded big business that stems either from antibusiness bias in the media or from inadequacies in journalists' understanding of corporate roles and goals.

The basic problem in media relations seems to be an intrinsic conflict of interest between publicists and journalists. Publicists seek maximum beneficial exposure for their clients, while journalists feel the pressure of a constant need for news yet are committed to the idea of an uninfluenced press. Reports and studies, most written by journalists, document the pervasive influence of big business on reporting of news and on media content as a whole. These writers defend the media in its attempts to avoid domination by business interests. Some researchers (for example, Gandy, entry 576) view the subject from a wider perspective. They question whether the standard public relations defense of media manipulation—that it is healthy for all views to be aired in a pluralistic society—deceives the public into believing that pluralism still applies, while in reality the power of managing the supply of information is increasingly concentrated in the hands of government and big business. Other observers focus on the press and its responsibilities in a free society. Here, corporate public relations personnel are generally viewed as the adversary, those who try to corrupt the free press. However, studies by third parties have concluded that the relationship between business and the press is mutually supportive, or at least symbiotic, with each side providing benefits to the other.

Subject headings to use in researching corporate media relations include Advertising, public service; Mass media and business; Press agents; Press releases; Promotion of special events; and Publicity.

391. Aronoff, Craig E., ed. **Business and the Media**. Proceedings of Business and the Media Symposium, Georgia State University, September 1977. Pacific Palisades, CA: Goodyear, 1979. 321 p. notes.

Twenty-three contributors representing business, the media, and public relations present a variety of views on how the media reports on business. Two sections consider the media's treatment of organized labor and media companies as profit-seeking entities.

392. Blohowiak, Donald W. **No Comment: An Executive's Essential Guide to the News Media**. New York: Praeger, 1987. 221 p. notes. bibliography.

Directed at corporate executives, this book is written in a popular style. The author, a public relations executive and former journalist, describes a one-way public relations communication model.

393. Evans, Fred J. **Managing the Media: Proactive Strategy for Better Business-Press Relations**. Westport, CT: Quorum, 1987. 172 p. bibliography.

Using a survey and interviews, the author (a former public affairs officer) examines the natural adversarial positions of the corporation and the journalist and discusses techniques for effective corporate use of the media. Case studies dealing with crisis communication, press strategies, and joint business-media programs are included.

394. Finn, David. **The Business-Media Relationship: Countering Misconceptions and Distrust**. An AMA Research Study. New York: American Management Association, 1981. 92 p.

Based on a survey of public relations executives and journalists, the author, a public relations practitioner, identifies problems of inaccurate reporting and lack of mutual understanding between these two groups. Six short case studies are included.

395. MacDougall, A. Kent. **Ninety Seconds to Tell It All: Big Business and the News Media**. Homewood, IL: Dow Jones-Irwin, 1981. 154 p. bibliography.

A general survey of the business-media relationship as seen in the major newspapers and television networks. Anecdotal examples are included, with particular attention given to coverage of nuclear power and environmental hazards.

396. McPhatter, William, ed. **The Business Beat: Its Impact and Its Problems**. ITT Key Issues Lecture Series. Indianapolis, IN: Bobbs-Merrill, 1980. 105 p.

Essays by two business representatives and four journalists, including one essay on public relations and the media. The press point of view is dominant in this collection.

397. Paletz, David L.; Pearson, Roberta E.; and Willis, Don L. **Politics in Public Service Advertising on Television**. New York: Praeger, 1977. 123 p. notes.

This scholarly study of the process and content of public service advertising examines the ways in which this communication attempts to influence public attitudes. Includes a description of the history and role of the Advertising Council.

GOVERNMENT RELATIONS

Government relations is an important aspect of corporate public relations, particularly in industries that are most affected by federal or state regulation. As corporations work to influence legislators and government agencies, directly and through grass-roots activity and industry associations, the Washington office becomes a critical contact point between top management and the outside world.

Government relations in general is the subject of the first list of materials in this section. It is followed by separate listings on the subjects of lobbying and political action committees. The general subject headings covering this topic include Corporations, U.S.--Political activity and Business and politics.

398. Braam, Geert P. A. **Influence of Business Firms on the Government: An Investigation of the Distribution of Influence in Society**. The Hague, Netherlands: Mouton, 1981. 320 p. notes. bibliography.

A scholarly Dutch study on the subject of influence relations. The author finds that the amount of influence a business has on government agencies is apparently related to business coalitions with interest-group support and to pressures from growing businesses; however, a direct correlation between amount of influence and firm size was not demonstrated. Although this is a Dutch study and the author was not concerned with studying the methods of influence used, the definition of influence in this work is quite similar to definitions of the aim of public relations.

399. Cigler, Allan J., and Loomis, Burdett A., eds. **Interest Group Politics**. 2d ed. Washington, DC: CQ Press, 1986. 319 p. notes.

Readings on instruments of political communication and influence, including PACs, campaign contributions, lobbying, and other interest-group activities.

400. Dominguez, George S. **Government Relations: A Handbook for Developing and Conducting the Company Program**. New York: Wiley, 1982. 420 p. bibliography.

A comprehensive guide for all aspects of corporate government relations, including organization of the function within the corporation. The author defines public relations in terms of tasks relating to the development and maintenance of external and internal relationships, while public affairs is viewed as the broader activity covering all aspects of company outreach programs.

401. Lusterman, Seymour. **Managing Business-State Government Relations**. Conference Board Report no. 838. New York: Conference Board, 1983. 59 p.

This report is based on a survey of companies, interviews, and a literature study. It includes a discussion of issues in the business-state interface, corporate political strategies, and the organization of this function within the corporation. Also by this author: *Managing Federal Government Relations* (Conference Board Report no. 905, 1988).

402. Lydenberg, Steven D. **Bankrolling Ballots: The Role of Business in Financing State Ballot Questions**. New York: Council on Economic Priorities, 1979. 90 p. notes.

403. Lydenberg, Steven D. **Bankrolling Ballots: Update 1980**. New York: Council on Economic Priorities, 1981. 200 p.

These two studies examine the effects of corporate and interest-group spending in 1978 and 1980 state and local campaigns on initiative and referendum questions. In both studies, the author finds that where corporations outspend their opponents by large amounts a measurable impact on voter attitudes is found; however, heavy spending does not assure victory.

404. McGrath, Phyllis S. **Redefining Corporate-Federal Relations**. Conference Board Report no. 757. New York: Conference Board, 1979. 102 p.

Based on information from a questionnaire and interviews, this study describes all areas of government-relations activity and includes sample job descriptions for the corporate function.

405. Moore, David G. **Politics and the Corporate Chief Executive**. Conference Board Report no. 777. New York: Conference Board, 1980. 50 p. notes.
Report of a survey on the political activity of chief executive officers.

406. Nadel, Mark V. **Corporations and Political Accountability**. Lexington, MA: Heath, 1976. 265 p. notes.
A scholarly study of corporate influence on public policy through campaign financing, lobbying, and pressure on government agencies. The author argues that corporations, by virtue of their size and power, are public entities and proposes means for reducing their power.

407. Ryan, Mike H.; Swanson, Carl L.; and Buchholz, Rogene A. **Corporate Strategy, Public Policy and the Fortune 500: How America's Major Corporations Influence Government**. New York: Oxford, 1987. 249 p. notes.
A scholarly study of corporations' strategic planning and their influence on the public policy process, based on analysis of corporate annual reports, PAC activity, and corporate violations of the law during the 1970s. Two chapters are devoted to the communication function of the annual report and two to PACs.

408. Shapiro, Irving S., with Kaufmann, Carl B. **America's Third Revolution: Public Interest and the Private Role**. New York: Harper, 1984. 283 p.
Examining corporate responses to government actions, the author (chief executive officer of the DuPont Corporation) documents the need for skilled external-affairs management in the corporation.

409. Shipper, Frank, and Jennings, Marianne M. **Business Strategy for the Political Arena**. Westport, CT: Quorum, 1984. 177 p. notes. bibliography.
A practical guide to the functions of the Washington office with emphasis on roles, tactics, and strategic planning. Also includes guidance on overseeing political action committees and responding to court actions.

410. Weidenbaum, Murray L. **Business, Government and the Public**. 3d ed. Englewood Cliffs, NJ: Prentice-Hall, 1986. 499 p. notes.
An overview of government policy toward business, its impact, and business responses; intended as a supplementary text for business students.

411. Weidenbaum, Murray L. **Future of Business Regulation: Private Action and Public Demand**. New York: Amacom, 1979. 183 p. notes.
The author looks at business, government, public interest groups, and the media in terms of their handling of regulatory issues and suggests how each group might modify its behavior.

Lobbying

Lobbying represents a special type of public relations communication. Milbrath (entry 32) describes lobbying as communication, by someone other than a private citizen, directed at government decision makers to influence their decisions. This activity, particularly at the national level, occupies a prominent place in most business-government public relations work. The Washington office is often the locus for activities designed to secure favorable treatment for the corporation. Such activities include planning and preparation for the corporate executive's visit to the Capitol, expert testimony before congressional groups, liaison activities with regulatory agencies, encouragement of grass-roots support for corporate political needs, and participation in industry-advocate organizations, such as trade associations. Washington representation for the corporation is often handled by a Washington, DC-based law firm or a public relations firm. The tasks of the Washington representative, according to Marcuss, are "finding the points of common interest, minimizing perceptions of conflict, mobilizing support and deflecting opposition" (entry 415, page xvi).

412.   Grefe, Edward A. **Fighting to Win: Business Political Power**. New York: Law & Business, 1981. 282 p. notes.

The subject of this work is grass-roots lobbying, especially by a corporation's employees. It includes an extensive appendix with guides for specific activities, job descriptions, surveys, and contracts. The author, an executive with Philip Morris, has excluded questions of morality and corporate social responsibility from consideration.

413.   Hayes, Michael T. **Lobbyists and Legislators: A Theory of Political Markets**. New Brunswick, NJ: Rutgers University Press, 1981. 200 p. notes. bibliography.

A scholarly theoretical study of the subject, including a literature survey.

414.   Levitan, Sar A., and Cooper, Martha R. **Business Lobbies: The Public Good and the Bottom Line**. Baltimore, MD: Johns Hopkins University Press, 1984. 154 p. notes.

The authors examine the major U.S. business lobbying organizations in their responses to issues of regulation and tax policy and include three case studies showing lobbying in action.

415.   Marcuss, Stanley J., ed. **Effective Washington Representation**. New York: Law & Business, 1983. 350 p. notes.

A practical and comprehensive guide to corporate lobbying describing specific communication situations and suggesting effective techniques for each.

416.   Moore, John L., ed. **The Washington Lobby**. 5th ed. Washington, DC: CQ Press, 1987. 212 p. bibliography.

A survey of lobbying by presidents, PACs, and interest groups, with case studies and a hstory of related legislation and court decisions.

For other books on this topic, *see* Cherington and Gillen, *The Business Representative in Washington* (entry 23); and Milbrath, *The Washington Lobbyists* (entry 32).

Political Action Committees

A recent type of business political activity is the development of political action committees (PACs), organizations that permit the corporation to contribute to political campaigns indirectly and legally. Studies that have attempted to assess the political power of PACs generally have been inconclusive regarding their effectiveness.

417. Alexander, Herbert E. **The Case for PACs**. A Public Affairs Council Monograph. Washington, DC: Public Affairs Council, 1983. 32 p.

A history and description of political action committees, with arguments in favor of PACs and suggestions for ways that their image can be improved.

418. Alexander, Herbert E., and Haggerty, Brian A. **PACs and Parties; Relationships and Interrelationships**. Report of a conference held May 22 and 23, 1984 in Washington, DC, sponsored by the Citizens' Research Foundation. Los Angeles: University of Southern California, 1984. 92 p. notes.

Brief summaries of the opinions expressed at this conference.

419. Fraser/Associates. **The PAC Handbook: Political Action for Business**. Cambridge, MA: Ballinger, 1980. 361 p. notes.

A partisan overview of PACs written in a popular style and including case studies.

420. Handler, Edward, and Mulkern, John R. **Business In Politics: Campaign Strategies of Corporate Political Action Committees**. Lexington, MA: Lexington, 1982. 128 p. notes. bibliography.

Based on interviews with PAC officers, this report focuses on fund raising techniques, spending, and internal operations during the 1978 and 1980 congressional elections.

421. Matasar, Ann B. **Corporate PACs and Federal Campaign Financing Laws: Use or Abuse of Power?** Westport, CT: Quorum, 1986. 161 p. notes. bibliography.

A guide for corporate PAC policymakers, using data from questionnaires, interviews, and filing documents and recommending more effective corporate utilization of PAC power.

422. Morrison, Catherine. **Managing Corporate Political Action Committees**. Conference Board Report no. 880. New York: Conference Board, 1986. 27 p.

A report of a survey of companies with and without PACs; includes a summary of PAC activity and administration.

423. Sabato, Larry J. **PAC Power: Inside the World of Political Action Committees**. New York: Norton, 1984. 251 p. notes. bibliography.

A comprehensive description of PAC development, operation, effectiveness, and possible future evolution based on a survey and interviews.

424. Sorauf, Frank J. **What Price PACs? Report**. New York: Twentieth Century Fund, 1984. 122 p. notes.

This background paper by the Twentieth Century Fund's Task Force on PACs describes the PAC phenomenon and presents options for reform.

PUBLIC RELATIONS AND CORPORATE PHILANTHROPY

Corporate philanthropic activities may be included within the scope of the public relations function. Certainly these programs contribute to the corporation's public image, although this effect may not be the primary goal of a philanthropic project. A Business

Roundtable document in 1981 stated that "All business entities should recognize philanthropy both as good business and as an obligation if they are to be considered responsible corporate citizens of the national and local communities in which they operate." (Business Roundtable's Position on Corporate Philanthropy, March 26, 1981; cited by Kathryn Troy in *The Corporate Contributions Function*, entry 432, p. 5). From this statement it is clear that philanthropy, community relations, and social responsibility are closely related topics.

Modern corporate philanthropy takes many forms, such as gifts to educational and cultural institutions, job-training programs, support of hospitals and community-service organizations, and even sponsorship of public television programming. The Conference Board has published a number of reports based on surveys of corporate activity in this area, and Human Resources Network has compiled a databank of these activities (*see* entry 380).

425. **Annual Survey of Corporate Contributions**. New York: Conference Board. (Annual)

Based on a survey of major U.S. corporations, this report describes trends in corporate giving and types of beneficiaries and includes a statistical profile of the year's activity.

426. Eells, Richard, ed. **International Business Philanthropy**. Columbia University, Graduate School of Business. Studies of the Modern Corporation. New York: Macmillan, 1979. 169 p. notes.

Papers from a 1976 symposium presenting the background, rationale, goals, and framework for international business philanthropy and public-service programs, especially in less-developed countries.

427. Fremont-Smith, Marion R. **Philanthropy and the Business Corporation**. New York: Russell Sage Foundation, 1972. 110 p. notes.

A somewhat critical historical study of corporate philanthropy programs, with suggestions for improvements.

428. Harris, James F., and Klepper, Anne. **Corporate Philanthropic Public Service Activities**. Conference Board Report no. 688. New York: Conference Board, 1976. 61 p. notes.

A survey of philanthropic activities in large corporations is analyzed, the findings are summarized, and recommendations regarding the appropriate level of corporate involvement, staffing, evaluation, and other areas are presented.

429. Koch, Frank. **The New Corporate Philanthropy: How Society and Business Can Profit**. New York: Plenum, 1979. 305 p. notes.

The author argues in favor of corporate philanthropic activities, describing the variety of potential recipient organizations and providing practical guidance on proposal evaluation and types of noncash assistance. Examples of philanthropic programs are included.

430. Lefever, Ernest W.; English, Raymond; and Schuettinger, Robert L. **Scholars, Dollars, and Public Policy: New Frontiers in Corporate Giving**. Washington, DC: Ethics and Public Policy Center, 1983. 63 p. notes.

A discussion of corporate support of nonprofit public policy groups, with guidelines for the selection of appropriate groups. Such support is a means of influencing government policy and countering antibusiness movements.

431. Mauksch, Mary. **Corporate Voluntary Contributions in Europe**. Conference Board Report no. 832. New York: Conference Board, 1982. 41 p.

Report of a survey of corporate activity in Great Britain and seven European countries.

432. Troy, Kathryn. **The Corporate Contributions Function**. Conference Board Report no. 820. New York: Conference Board, 1982. 39 p. notes.

A profile, based on a survey, of large corporations' corporate-contributions offices and their work.

433. Troy, Kathryn. **Managing Corporate Contributions**. Conference Board Report no. 792. New York: Conference Board, 1980. 95 p. bibliography.

A concise guide to the management of direct giving and cosponsored foundations, describing planning, goal setting, organization, budgeting, and evaluation.

PUBLIC RELATIONS AND CORPORATE SOCIAL RESPONSIBILITY

A growing body of literature in the field of business administration is concerned with the topic of corporate social responsibility. Although most of it is not written by or for public relations specialists, this material is relevant to the study of corporate public relations. A large segment of the American public is disinclined these days to accept the old adage what is good for General Motors is good for America. The public relations function of managing and monitoring the communication process between business and society ("good deeds made known") takes on increased status when corporate management adopts a socially responsible stance and makes a commitment to social concerns as a goal equal in importance to the maximizing of profits.

Subject headings for locating material on this topic include Corporations--Social aspects and Industry--Social aspects.

434. Anshen, Melvin. **Corporate Strategies for Social Performance**. Columbia University, Graduate School of Business. Studies of the Modern Corporation. New York: Macmillan, 1980. 274 p. notes.

Suggesting that modern corporations have no choice but to become involved in social issues, the author examines planning and implementation issues and describes the enlarged role of public relations in the management of external relations.

435. Anshen, Melvin, ed. **Managing the Socially Responsible Corporation**. The 1972-73 Paul Garrett Lectures. Columbia University, Graduate School of Business. Studies of the Modern Corporation. New York: Macmillan, 1974. 206 p. notes.

The focus of these lectures is how business can respond to demands for socially responsible behavior. Includes a lecture by Harold Burson of Burson, Marsteller on the public relations function in corporations.

436. Bradshaw, Thornton, and Vogel, David, eds. **Corporations and Their Critics: Issues and Answers to the Problems of Corporate Social Responsibility**. New York: McGraw-Hill, 1981. 285 p. notes.

A selection of essays, some written by representatives of companies with successful social-responsibility programs and some by outside observers of these developments. Topics addressed include programs for consumers, employees, and stockholders; corporate philanthropy; press relations; and political activity.

437. Buchholz, Rogene A. **Business Environment and Public Policy: Implications for Management**. Englewood Cliffs, NJ: Prentice-Hall, 1982. 542 p. bibliographies.

A text for future managers presenting an overview of corporate public policy concerns. It includes discussion of corporate social responsibility, issues management, the social audit, business-government relations, and corporate-structure changes for more effective public policy response.

438. Carroll, Archie B., ed. **Managing Corporate Social Responsibility**. Boston: Little, Brown, 1977. 351 p. notes.

A selection of readings, most from academic management journals of the mid-1970s, that start with the presumption that business has a social responsibility and consider how this function is implemented in the modern corporation. Two recurring themes are the need for top-management commitment and the importance of communication skills.

439. Chamberlain, Neil W. **Social Strategy and Corporate Structure**. Columbia University, Graduate School of Business. Studies of the Modern Corporation. New York: Macmillan, 1982. 169 p. notes.

Suggestions for corporate restructuring to allow more effective response to the changing social environment. No direct reference to public relations but useful for background reading.

440. Cohn, Jules. **The Conscience of the Corporations: Business and Urban Affairs, 1967-1970**. Baltimore, MD: Johns Hopkins University Press, 1971. 122 p. bibliography.

Based on a national study, this work analyzes the corporate role in relieving urban problems, giving special attention to job problems for the disadvantaged. Organization of the urban-affairs function is also discussed.

441. Lydenberg, Steven D., et al. **Rating America's Corporate Conscience: A Provocative Guide to the Companies behind the Products You Buy Every Day**. Reading, MA: Addison-Wesley for the Council on Economic Priorities, 1986. 499 p. notes.

Descriptive profiles of one hundred thirty providers of consumer goods, rated according to their performance in such areas as charitable contributions, corporate social disclosure, and representation of women and minorities in management.

442. Miles, Robert H. **Managing the Corporate Social Environment: A Grounded Theory**. Englewood Cliffs, NJ: Prentice-Hall, 1987. 319 p. notes. bibliography.

Using the insurance industry as an example, the author identifies factors in the corporate structure and industrial context that affect the effectiveness of external-affairs management programs.

443. Rowtow, Jerome M., ed. **Views from the Top: Establishing the Foundation for the Future of Business**. New York: Facts on File, 1985. 207 p.

Nine chief executive officers address topics relating to the present and future role of the corporation in society, including reshaping the organization, strategic planning, managing people, and creating the corporate culture.

444. Sethi, S. Prakash, ed. **The Unstable Ground: Corporate Social Policy in a Dynamic Society**. Los Angeles: Melville, 1974. 557 p. bibliographies.

Papers from a 1972 symposium present views of representatives of business and society on the question of corporate social responsibility and how it might be implemented.

445. Spitzer, Carlton E. **Raising the Bottom Line: Business Leadership in a Changing Society**. Longman Series in Public Communication. White Plains, NY: Longman, 1982. 226 p.

In short essays written in a readable style, the author looks at examples of business-government communication and cooperation and expresses optimism about corporate acceptance of social responsibility.

446. Vogel, David. **Lobbying the Corporation: Citizen Challenges to Business Authority**. New York: Basic, 1978. 270 p. notes.

The author examines the effects of shareholder and consumer activism on corporations and their public relations programs.

The Corporate Social Audit

The corporate social audit, a concept developed in the early 1970s, is a tool for evaluating a corporation's responsiveness to the needs of its publics. It has been described as a "systematic attempt to identify, analyze, measure, evaluate and monitor the effect of an organization's operations on society and on the public well-being." (Blake, entry 450, p. 3.)

The subject is represented in Library of Congress catalog systems by the heading Social accounting.

447. Abt, Clark C. **The Social Audit for Management**. New York: Amacom, 1977. 278 p. bibliography.

This is a thorough examination of the subject, written for corporate and government officials and the general public by a consultant who specializes in preparing social audits. It includes case studies, a review of the corporate-social-audit literature, and the history of the social-research industry.

448. American Institute of Certified Public Accountants, Committee on Social Measurement. **Measurement of Corporate Social Performance: Determining the Impact of Business Actions on Areas of Social Concern.** New York: AICPA, 1977. 355 p. bibliography.

This study describes how to collect data, what to measure, and appropriate forms for public reporting.

449. Bauer, Raymond A., and Fenn, Dan H., Jr. **The Corporate Social Audit.** Social Science Frontiers no. 5. New York: Russell Sage Foundation, 1972. 102 p. notes. bibliography.

The social audit is defined here as the comprehensive and continuing evaluation of the social performance of firms. The authors, among the first to suggest the concept, examine the development and future of social auditing, calling for further research on the quantification of social costs.

450. Blake, David H.; Frederick, William C.; and Myers, Mildred S. **Social Auditing: Evaluating the Impact of Corporate Programs.** New York: Praeger, 1976. 168 p. bibliography.

Written for scholars and management personnel, this study defines types of social audits and describes their uses.

451. Corson, John J., and Steiner, George A. **Measuring Business's Social Performance: The Corporate Social Audit.** New York: Committee on Economic Development, 1974. 75 p. notes.

Report on a survey of types of corporate social audits and their uses.

452. Task Force on Corporate Social Performance. **Corporate Social Reporting in the United States and Western Europe.** Washington, DC: U.S. Department of Commerce, 1979. 177 p. bibliography.

Based on a survey of major American and Western European corporations, this is a comprehensive review of types, audiences, and uses of social audits, with several extensive examples.

INTERNATIONAL PUBLIC RELATIONS

While public relations is in some respects a peculiarly American phenomenon, it has spread, along with the multinational corporation, to most parts of the world. The Public Relations World Congress meets every three years in different countries, under the auspices of the International Public Relations Association, to examine professional questions on an international level. Recent meetings of this body include the eighth, held in London in 1979 (*see* entry 4); the ninth, held in 1982 in Bombay; the 1985 meeting in Amsterdam; and the 1988 meeting in Melbourne, Australia. IPRA Gold Papers have been published since 1973 in conjunction with these meetings.

Relevant subject headings for this topic include Corporations, international--Public opinion and International business enterprises--Public relations.

453. Basche, James R., Jr. **U.S. Business Support for International Public Service Activities**. New York: Conference Board, 1973-1975. In six parts. Part 1: "Support from U.S. Headquarters," 1973, report no. 593. Parts 2-6: "Support from Foreign Affiliates:" (Brazil, 1974, report no. 616; Mexico, 1974, report no. 617; Argentina, 1974, report no. 624; Colombia, 1974, report no. 643; The Philippines, 1975, report no. 657).

Program objectives (including image building), criteria and evaluation, and suggestions for improvement are reported. Types of programs include educational and research, health and welfare, business education, athletics, civic activity, the arts, and exchange programs.

454. Blake, David H. **Managing the External Relations of Multinational Corporations**. New York: Fund for Multinational Management, 1977. 100 p. notes. bibliography.

The author surveys the particular functions of corporate public relations in multinational situations. Topics considered include institutionalizing the public affairs function, involvement in planning and forecasting, organizational issues, and performance of subsidiaries.

455. Business International. **Corporate External Affairs: Blueprint for Survival**. Research Report 75-4. Geneva: Business International, 1975. 146 p.

Based on an interview project of Professor J. J. Boddewyn, this study of corporate relations with governmental and other official bodies presents examples of corporate policies, mainly from European multinationals.

456. Currah, Philip. **Setting Up a European Public Relations Operation**. London: Business Books, 1975. 225 p. bibliography.

Published in cooperation with the Institute of Public Relations, this is a practical introductory guide to the topic.

457. Dunn, S. Watson; Cahill, Martin F.; and Boddewyn, Jean J. **How Fifteen Transnational Corporations Manage Public Affairs**. Chicago: Crain, 1979. 115 p.

Case studies are used to illustrate some of the problems peculiar to international corporate management, for example, the effects of local business practices, cultural differences, and host-government objectives.

458. Hill & Knowlton. **Handbook on International Public Relations**. Vol. 1, **Western Europe**. Vol. 2, **Australia, Hong Kong, India, Japan, Latin America, Malaysia, New Zealand, Singapore**. New York: Praeger, 1967-1968. Vol. 1, 202 p. Vol. 2, 154 p.

Public relations specialists in each country wrote the chapters in this practical and comprehensive work, now in need of updating.

459. Janger, Allen R., and Berenbeim, Ronald E. **External Challenges to Management Decisions: A Growing International Business Problem**. Conference Board Report no. 808. New York: Conference Board, 1981. 68 p.

Using examples from six countries, this report describes interest-group pressures and the ways in which corporations have attempted to communicate with these groups.

460. Lusterman, Seymour. **Managing International Public Affairs**. Conference Board Report no. 861. New York: Conference Board, 1985. 34 p.

A survey of the use of international public affairs specialists in corporations, including identification of trends and problems.

461. McGuire, E. Patrick. **Corporate Aid Programs in Twelve Less-Developed Countries**. Conference Board Report no. 834. New York: Conference Board, 1983. 43 p. notes.

Report of a joint Conference Board-Agency for International Development study examining employee health and educational programs and community-assistance activities, with examples from a number of Third World countries.

462. Ricks, David R. **Big Business Blunders: Mistakes in Multinational Marketing**. Homewood, IL: Dow Jones-Irwin, 1983. 158 p. bibliography.

Examples provided here include faulty adaptation of products for foreign markets, poor name choices, promotion mistakes, translation errors, and other cases in which cultural differences presented barriers to communication.

463. Roth, Robert F. **International Marketing Communications**. Chicago: Crain, 1982. 353 p. notes. bibliography.

A practical guide for managers, also intended as a text. Public relations is defined in the context of the marketing mix as promoting continued awareness of the company and product.

APPLICATIONS IN PARTICULAR INDUSTRIES

The titles listed here describe appropriate public relations programs for companies and organizations within specific industries. Works on public relations activities in industries not listed here may be located by searching in library catalogs or records of published titles, such as *Cumulative Book Index* or *Bibliographic Index* (entry 286), under the subject heading Public relations--(name of industry). Refer to chapter 7 for material on public relations in nonprofit institutions.

Accounting

464. American Institute of Certified Public Accountants. **Public Relations Guide for CPAs**. New York: AICPA, Public Relations Division, 1984. 39 p. bibliography.

A brief summary of practical information.

Entertainment Industry

465. O'Brien, Richard. **Publicity: How to Get It**. New York: Harper, 1977. 176 p.

A practical work limited to publicity activities and written by a publicist working in this industry. See also Rein, et al., *High Visibility* (entry 16).

Financial Services

466. Troy, Kathryn. **Public Affairs in Financial Services**. Conference Board Report no. 899. New York: Conference Board, 1987. 41 p. notes.

The author examines how banks, insurance companies, and diversified financial corporations have responded to negative publicity in recent years. She describes the functions of the public affairs officer in this industry.

Forest Industries

467. Rich, Stuart U., ed. **Public Relations in an Era of Public Involvement: Challenge for the Timber Industry**. Proceedings of Second Current Issues Conference, Portland, Oregon, March 22, 1973. Eugene, OR: University of Oregon College of Business Administration, Forest Industries Center, 1973. 104 p.

Papers on the public relations issues and problems faced by managers in forest and land-management industries by conference participants representing public relations practice, the U.S. Forest Service, the news media, and academia.

Public Utilities

468. Sullivan, Frank C. **Crisis of Confidence: Utilities, Public Relations and Credibility**. Canaan, NH: Phoenix, 1977. 129 p. notes.

An examination of the problems faced by public utilities in the 1970s as an example of the problems of business in general. Topics include rate setting, lobbying, affirmative action, and environmentalism. The treatment is general with very few specific examples.

Services

469. Webb, Stanley G. **Marketing and Strategic Planning for Professional Service Firms**. New York: Amacom, 1982. 293 p.

Public relations activities are included in the marketing framework in this work for managers of professional services.

5

Public Relations in Government

The work of the public relations specialist is evident in most activities of federal and state agencies. However, because the use of "publicity experts" in the federal government without a specific congressional appropriation for that purpose has been forbidden since 1913, government employees with this function go by other names: press secretary and public affairs or public information officer are the most common titles used. Government agencies with large numbers of such specialists include the United States Information Agency, the Defense Department, and the Department of Health and Human Services. However, personnel performing public relations functions are found in almost all government agencies and departments.

Although the primary function of public relations in government is to communicate information about government programs to the public, Altheide and Johnson have noted that official reports of government agencies may be generated primarily for the purpose of promoting the agency and/or maintaining its legitimacy (entry 1). Such reports do not necessarily represent an unbiased presentation of facts.

This chapter begins with the subject of political communication theory. Works on the practice of public relations in government comprise the next section, followed by studies and reports on relations between the news media and government departments. The chapter concludes with a list of titles describing public relations activity in the White House.

POLITICAL COMMUNICATION

Formal study of political communication is a fairly recent phenomenon. The term began to appear in indexes to the social-science literature around 1975. The American Institute for Political Communication, founded in the 1960s and no longer in existence, included on its board of directors several prominent academics and former corporate executives; it published several studies on government communication and the *Political Communication Bulletin* (entry 233) during the 1960s and early 1970s.

Political communication appears as a subject heading in some political-science bibliographies and indexes but is not generally used elsewhere. The Library of Congress subject headings for material on this topic are Propaganda, Communication in politics, and Public relations and politics.

470. Chafee, Steven H., ed. **Political Communication: Issues and Strategies for Research**. Sage Annual Reviews of Communication Research, vol. 4. Newbury Park, CA: Sage, 1975. 319 p. notes.

A scholarly review of the current state of research on the subjects of election campaigning, government-media relations, and the media's role in political agenda setting.

471.   Kaid, Lynda L.; Nimmo, Dan D.; and Sanders, Keith R., eds. **New Perspectives on Political Advertising**. Political Communication Yearbook. Carbondale, IL: Southern Illinois University Press, 1986. 370 p. notes.

The contributors to this volume examine aspects of campaign and corporate advocacy advertising, with emphasis on the television medium. Two of the articles deal with British and Australian practices.

472.   Nimmo, Dan D., and Combs, James E. **Subliminal Politics: Myths and Mythmakers in America**. Englewood Cliffs, NJ: Prentice-Hall, 1980. 256 p. notes.

A view of American society and politics in terms of the myths that shape our perceptions; includes a chapter (mostly derogatory) on the practice of public relations.

473.   Nimmo, Dan D., and Sanders, Keith R., eds. **Handbook of Political Communication**. Newbury Park, CA: Sage, 1981. 732 p. notes. bibliographies.

A collection of articles on the content and method of contemporary political communication research, well-footnoted and including two bibliographic essays.

474.   Rasberry, Robert W. **The Technique of Political Lying**. Lanham, MD: University Press of America, 1981. 289 p. bibliography.

Application of a theory of propaganda proposed by Jacques Ellul to the events of Watergate.

475.   Sanders, Keith R.; Kaid, Lynda L.; and Nimmo, Dan D., eds. **Political Communication Yearbook**. Carbondale, IL: Southern Illinois University Press, 1985. 358 p. bibliography.

The contributors to this volume review theory, current topics in the field, and recent research. An extensive bibliography is included.

476.   Yudof, Mark G. **When Government Speaks: Politics, Law and Government Expression in America**. Berkeley, CA: University of California Press, 1983. 323 p. notes.

A legal scholar's examination of government communications and First Amendment constraints on secrecy and censorship.

PRACTICAL WORKS FOR GOVERNMENT OFFICIALS

477.   Arnold, David S.; Becker, Christine S.; and Kellar, Elizabeth K., eds. **Effective Communication: Getting the Message Across**. Washington, DC: International City Management Association, 1983. 229 p. bibliography.

Public communication guidelines for local government employees; apparently an update of Gilbert's 1975 *Public Relations in Local Government* (entry 480), but with a slightly different focus.

478.   Eppley, Garrett G. **Improve Your Public Relations: With the Three A's as Your Guide**. Arlington, VA: National Recreation and Park Association, 1977. 172 p. bibliography.

A text for a recreation or parks administration course, this is a practical introductory work. The author is an educator and experienced recreation administrator.

479. Fazio, James R., and Gilbert, Douglas L. **Public Relations and Communications for Natural Resource Managers**. 2d ed. Dubuque, IA: Kendall/Hunt, 1986. 399 p. notes. bibliography.

A thorough introduction to the particular public relations challenges of natural-resources management. Interpretation and conservation as well as environmental education aspects are included in this work, which is intended for use as a text and includes chapter readings and a useful six-page bibliography.

480. Gilbert, William H., ed. **Public Relations in Local Government**. Washington, DC: International City Management Association for the Institute for Training in Municipal Administration, 1975. 266 p. notes. bibliography.

An overview of practical public relations for municipal officials and employees, intended for in-service training programs. A suggested code of ethics for municipal officers and employees is included. *See* entry 477.

481. Helm, Louis M., et al., eds. **Informing the People: A Public Affairs Handbook**. Longman Series in Public Communication. White Plains, NY: Longman, 1981. 359 p. notes. bibliography.

A guidebook for government information personnel that includes historical and legal aspects, communication theory, techniques, and practices.

482. Mater, Jean. **Public Hearings, Procedures and Strategies: A Guide to Influencing Public Decisions**. Englewood Cliffs, NJ: Prentice-Hall, 1984. 271 p. notes.

A practical guide to holding and participating in public hearings for officials and the general public.

483. Mokwa, Michael P., and Permit, Steven E., eds. **Government Marketing: Theory and Practice**. Papers from an American Marketing Association Conference and Workshop, Yale University, May 1979. New York: Praeger, 1981. 384 p. notes.

Government public information presented from a marketing perspective for students, agency officials, and scholars.

PUBLIC INFORMATION OFFICES IN ACTION

The following list includes studies and reports on the activities of all types of government public relations offices and officials, except the president and White House. Several of these studies examine the dissemination of information in the military sector. Some works treating foreign government communications are also included.

Because the government, like the private sector, depends on mass-media channels to transmit its messages, many of these works focus on the relationships of government officials and the media. One recurrent theme in this literature is government withholding of information and manipulation of the news. Another area of interest is the pack-like behavior of reporters, which results, in part, from the technical impossibility of covering all parts of the massive government bureaucracy. The extent of journalistic freedom from political pressure in presenting the news has been studied, by Hess, Paletz and others (*see* entries 499-501 and 509).

Subject headings that are useful in providing access to these topics include Government publicity, Government information, Government and the press, Government advertising, and Official secrets.

484. American Institute for Political Communication. **The Credibility Problem**. Washington, DC: AIPC, 1972. 84 p.

A study of the interactions between government officials and the news media during the Nixon administration, with an examination of the public information function. An earlier study by this organization, *The Federal Government-Daily Press Relationship* (1966), reported on the roles of government and press in reporting on public issues during the Kennedy administration. *See* entry 542 for a more recent study by AIPC on the relationship between the Nixon administration and the mass media during the 1972 presidential campaign.

485. Berkson, Larry C. **The Supreme Court and Its Publics: The Communication of Policy Decisions**. Lexington, MA: Lexington, 1978. 145 p. notes.

The author, a political scientist, suggests ways in which access to decisions can be improved and deals briefly with the role of the public information officer.

486. Blanchard, Robert O., ed. **Congress and the News Media**. Studies in Public Communication. New York: Hastings, 1974. 506 p. notes. bibliography.

A set of edited reprints (including historical documents), studies of interactions between Congress and the media, editorials, speeches, and an excerpt from a publication for members of Congress on how to handle their own public relations.

487. Braestrup, Peter. **Battle Lines: Background Paper. Report of the Twentieth Century Fund Task Force on the Military and the Media**. New York: Priority Press, 1985. 178 p. notes.

This background paper provides an overview of military-press relations since 1941 and identifies as issues the freedom of the press, dissemination of misleading information, and cultural clashes between military and media.

488. Brasch, Walter M., and Ulloth, Dana R., eds. **The Press and the State: Socio-Historical and Contemporary Studies**. Lanham, MD: University Press of America, 1986. 811 p. notes.

A comprehensive survey on a general topic, with one section on the state as manipulator of public information; includes reprints of significant historical articles.

489. Chittick, William O. **The State Department, Press and Pressure Groups: A Role Analysis**. Wiley Series on Government and Communication. New York: Wiley, 1970. 373 p. notes.

A research study of the reasons for conflict among these three groups, focusing on differences in role perceptions and expectations.

490. Firestone, O. J. **The Public Persuader: Government Advertising**. Toronto: Methuen, 1970. 258 p. notes.

A Canadian study of government advertising—its objectives, types, problems, and the role of agencies.

491. Fixx, James F., ed. **The Mass Media and Politics**. New York: Arno Press, 1972. 636 p. bibliography.

Selected articles from *The New York Times*, 1936 to 1971, illustrating the history of the media-politics connection.

492. Fulbright, James W. **The Pentagon Propaganda Machine**. New York: Liveright, 1970. 166 p.

The author presents evidence to support his thesis that the Pentagon uses its public information mandate for self-promotion.

493. Galnoor, Itzhak, ed. **Government Secrecy in Democracies**. New York: New York University Press, 1977. 317 p. notes.

Essays by political science and public administration scholars on government secrecy and symbolic uses of information in ten countries.

494. Goodsell, Charles T., ed. **The Public Encounter: Where State and Citizen Meet**. Bloomington, IN: Indiana University Press, 1981. 267 p. notes. bibliography.

Written for scholars and the general public, this volume presents predominantly theoretical perspectives, most from political scientists, analyzing the areas of citizen-government interaction.

495. Goulding, Phil G. **Confirm or Deny: Informing the People on National Security**. New York: Harper, 1970. 369 p.

A descriptive study of selected public relations crisis situations in the Department of Defense between 1965 and 1968, during which time the author served as assistant secretary of defense for public affairs.

496. Halberstam, David. **The Powers That Be**. New York: Knopf, 1979. 771 p. bibliography.

A study of four major news organs (two newspapers, a news magazine, and one television network), showing how modern media shape our perceptions of political events.

497. Harris, Robert. **Gotcha! The Media, the Government and the Falklands Crisis**. London: Faber & Faber, 1983. 158 p.

A journalist's account of the British government's mishandling of information about the Falklands War.

498. Heise, Juergen A. **Minimum Disclosure: How the Pentagon Manipulates the News**. New York: Norton, 1979. 221 p. notes.

From an examination of the Pentagon's handling of bad news, the author recommends a redefining of the government public information officer's role and better educating of top military officers on their responsibilities to the public.

499. Hess, Stephen. **The Government/Press Connection: Press Officers and Their Offices**. Newswork series, vol. 2. Washington, DC: Brookings, 1984. 160 p.

An account based on direct observation of the press officers in U.S. government agencies, departments, and the White House. Second volume in the author's Newswork series, along with *The Ultimate Insiders* (entry 500) and *The Washington Reporters* (entry 501).

500. Hess, Stephen. **The Ultimate Insiders: U.S. Senators in the National Media**. Newswork series, vol. 3. Washington, DC: Brookings, 1986. 151 p. notes.

This volume examines the determinants of media coverage of members of the Senate. One chapter describes how legislators and their press secretaries court the media.

501. Hess, Stephen. **The Washington Reporters**. Newswork series, vol. 1. Washington, DC: Brookings, 1981. 174 p. notes.

A descriptive study of the composition and behavior of the Washington press corps. In this and other Newswork studies, the author's sources include interviews, previous studies, and news archives.

502. Hiebert, Ray E., and Spitzer, Carlton E. **The Voice of Government**. New York: Wiley, 1968. 354 p. bibliography.

An introduction, for students and citizens, to the public information function in government.

503. Holmes, Deborah. **Governing the Press: Media Freedom in the U.S. and Great Britain**. Boulder, CO: Westview, 1986. 107 p. bibliography.

A comparison of press freedom and prestige in the two countries, noting the relative freedom of the press in the United States and the resulting prevalence of government manipulation of the media. The author uses as examples the reporting of the Falklands story in the British media and the Iran hostage crisis in the American press.

504. Kail, F. M. **What Washington Said: American Rhetoric and the Vietnam War, 1949-1969**. New York: Harper, 1973. 248 p. notes.

A study of political rhetoric based on official reports printed in *The New York Times*.

505. MacDonald, J. Fred. **Television and the Red Menace: The Video Road to Vietnam**. New York: Praeger, 1985. 277 p. bibliography.

A scholarly examination of television as a medium for government propaganda over the past forty years. The author believes that television has become more committed to balanced reporting in recent years.

506. Minor, Dale. **The Information War**. New York: Hawthorn Books, 1970. 212 p. notes.

A general examination of the ways in which the news media are manipulated and controlled by external and internal forces.

507. Morgan, David. **The Capitol Press Corps: Newsmen and the Governing of New York State**. Westport, CT: Greenwood, 1978. 177 p. notes. bibliography.

A study of the problems of reporting state news, including discussion of the role of the press aide/public information officer. The author identifies shortcomings in the performance of both press aides and news reporters.

508. Morgan, David. **The Flacks of Washington: Government Information and the Public Agenda**. Westport, CT: Greenwood, 1986. 165 p. bibliography.

On the basis of evidence collected from interviews of Washington reporters and government information officers, the author concludes that both groups' output should be treated with skepticism. Special attention is given to the air traffic controllers' strike.

509. Paletz, David L., and Entman, Robert M. **Media Power Politics**. New York: Free Press, 1981. 308 p. notes. bibliography.

A scholarly study of the power of the media in American society and the manipulation of this power source by government leaders, officials, and interest groups. The powers responsible for manipulating the media are identified and described, and the effects on public opinion and political participation are examined.

510. Rivers, William L. **The Adversaries: Politics and the Press**. Boston: Beacon, 1970. 273 p.

In anecdotal style, the author describes the adversarial position of press and government, a relationship that he believes is necessary for maintaining accountability in government. Rivers' coverage of this topic began with his 1969 volume *The Opinion Makers*.

511. Rivers, William L. **The Other Government: Power and the Washington Media**. New York: Universe, 1982. 240 p.

Rivers, in a popular style, provides a useful introduction to the world of Washington news bureaus and correspondents.

512. Sigal, Leon V. **Reporters and Officials: The Organization and Politics of Newsmaking**. Lexington, MA: Heath, 1973. 221 p. bibliography.

The author examines the interactions between news reporters and public officials and documents instances of news management by government.

513. Small, William J. **Political Power and the Press**. New York: Norton, 1972. 423 p.

An examination of government interference in news reporting, written by a strong advocate of a free press.

514. Steinberg, Charles S. **The Information Establishment: Our Government and the Media**. New York: Hastings, 1980. 366 p. bibliography.

A general overview of government-media relations covering the White House, executive departments and agencies, and Congress. The author examines the interdependencies of government bodies and the media and how their respective needs are satisfied. The activities of the National News Council are described.

515. Wise, David. **The Politics of Lying: Government Deception, Secrecy and Power**. New York: Random House, 1973. 415 p.

A general overview in a journalistic style, based on interviews with government officials.

See also Hiebert, *The Press in Washington* (entry 27); Nimmo, *Newsgathering in Washington* (entry 33); and Pimlott, *Public Relations and American Democracy* (entry 35).

PRESIDENTIAL PUBLIC RELATIONS

Relations between presidents and representatives of the press have attracted considerable attention, both in the news media and in published memoirs and studies of the type listed below. The advent of television and its extensive use by some presidents has reduced the power of the press as intermediary between the president and the public. In addition, television events, such as presidential debates, have suggested that image is more powerful than rational ideas in communication with viewers.

516.   Deakin, James. **Straight Stuff: The Reporters, the White House and the Truth**. New York: Morrow, 1984. 378 p. notes.
A personal memoir by a White House reporter who worked from the period of the Eisenhower administration to Reagan's presidency.

517.   Denton, Robert E., Jr., and Hahn, Dan F. **Presidential Communication: Description and Analysis**. New York: Praeger, 1986. 332 p. notes. bibliographies.
An overview documenting the rise of the "rhetorical" presidency and applying a wide range of communications research to the subject. Suggested additional readings are provided with each chapter.

518.   Gallagher, Hugh G. **FDR's Splendid Deception**. New York: Dodd, Mead, 1985. 250 p. bibliography.
How the president maintained his image and minimized public perception of his physical disability.

519.   Graber, Doris A., ed. **The President and the Public**. Philadelphia, PA: Institute for the Study of Human Issues, 1982. 310 p. bibliography.
An anthology of studies of the presidential image, campaign issues, and public appraisals of presidential performance.

520.   Grossman, Michael B., and Kumar, Martha J. **Portraying the President: The White House and the News Media**. Baltimore, MD: Johns Hopkins University Press, 1981. 358 p. notes.
A study of White House-press relations based on research during the Ford and Carter presidencies.

521.   Hagerty, James C. **The Diary of James C. Hagerty: Eisenhower in Mid-course, 1954-55**. Edited by Robert H. Ferrell. Bloomington, IN: Indiana University Press, 1983. 269 p. notes.
A first-hand account by one of the most successful presidential press secretaries. Includes discussion of the role of television during this period and the fall of Senator McCarthy.

522.   Juergens, George. **News from the White House: The Presidential-Press Relationship in the Progressive Era**. Chicago: University of Chicago Press, 1981. 338 p. bibliography.
A historical study beginning with Theodore Roosevelt's presidency and ending with Woodrow Wilson. The author notes the emergence of the modern presidency and the professionalization of Washington reporters during this period.

523.   Keogh, James. **President Nixon and the Press**. New York: Funk & Wagnalls, 1972. 212 p.
A reporter and member of the presidential staff describes the growth of press power and arrogance.

524.   Kern, Montague; Levering, Patricia W.; and Levering, Ralph B. **The Kennedy Crisis: The Press, the Presidency and Foreign Policy**. Chapel Hill, NC: University of North Carolina Press, 1983. 290 p. bibliography.
Using content analysis of five newspapers plus interviews, the authors study presidential and other influences on the reporting of major foreign policy issues.

525.   Kernell, Samuel. **Going Public: New Strategies of Presidential Leadership**. Washington, DC: CQ Press, 1986. 251 p. notes.
A selective examination of presidents from Roosevelt to Reagan, focusing on their efforts to transform personal public support into policy support.

526.   Klein, Herbert G. **Making It Perfectly Clear**. Garden City, NY: Doubleday, 1980. 464 p.
The personal memoir of President Nixon's public relations advisor and director of communications, chronicling the communication between the White House and the media.

527.   Lang, Gladys E., and Lang, Kurt. **The Battle for Public Opinion: The President, the Press, and the Polls During Watergate**. New York: Columbia University Press, 1983. 353 p. notes.
A study of Nixon's adversarial relationship with the press and its effect on news reporting and on public opinion.

528.   Lashner, Marilyn A. **The Chilling Effect in TV News: Intimidation by the Nixon White House**. New York: Praeger, 1984. 296 p. bibliography.
Comparing television and newspaper political news commentary, the author finds that the regulatory policies affecting television broadcasting inhibit network news commentaries.

529.   Nessen, Ron. **It Sure Looks Different from the Inside**. New York: Playboy Press, 1978. 367 p.
A journalistic description of the experience of a former newsman who became press secretary to Gerald Ford.

530.   Orman, John M. **Presidential Secrecy and Deception: Beyond the Power to Persuade**. Westport, CT: Greenwood, 1980. 239 p. bibliography.
A study of secrecy and press manipulation in administrations from Kennedy to Ford, with a call for presidential accountability.

531.   Porter, William E. **Assault on the Media: The Nixon Years**. Ann Arbor, MI: University of Michigan Press, 1976. 320 p. notes.
An account of executive-branch actions affecting media freedom between 1969 and 1974, including texts of significant documents.

532.   Seymour-Ure, Colin. **The American President: Power and Communication**. New York: St. Martin, 1982. 190 p. notes.

A study of the communication techniques of presidents since 1945, with emphasis on Eisenhower and Nixon.

533.   Spear, Joseph C. **Presidents and the Press: The Nixon Legacy**. Cambridge, MA: MIT Press, 1984. 349 p. notes.

A journalistic account of presidential manipulation of the press as practiced by Nixon.

534.   Spragens, William C., with Terwoord, Carole. **From Spokesman to Press Secretary: White House Media Operations**. Lanham, MD: University Press of America, 1981. 243 p.

A historical survey of presidential press secretaries from Hagerty to Powell, categorizing them as technicians or policy advisors and showing how the confidence of the president was a necessary factor in their effectiveness.

535.   Thompson, Kenneth W., ed. **Three Press Secretaries on the Presidency and the Press: Jody Powell, George Reedy, and Jerry terHorst**. Markle Foundation Series, vol. 5. Lanham, MD: University Press of America, 1983. 113 p.

First-hand reports on the role of the presidential press secretary. This series includes other volumes in addition to the two cited here, all concerned with presidential communication styles and techniques.

536.   Thompson, Kenneth W., ed. **The White House Press on the Presidency: News Management and Co-option**. Markle Foundation Series, vol. 4. Lanham, MD: University Press of America, 1983. 81 p.

Descriptive accounts and transcribed conversations of three White House reporters (Frank Cormier, James Deakin, and Helen Thomas) on the subject of presidential press conferences.

537.   Turner, Kathleen J. **Lyndon Johnson's Dual War: Vietnam and the Press**. Chicago: University of Chicago Press, 1985. 358 p. bibliography.

A detailed examination of President Johnson's relationship with the press and his Vietnam War rhetoric, with particular attention to his communication failures.

538.   White, Graham J. **FDR and the Press**. Chicago: University of Chicago Press, 1979. 186 p. notes.

A revision of the author's dissertation, this examination of press-conference transcripts and other contemporary documents describes and analyzes Roosevelt's press relations. Two chapters deal specifically with his handling of Washington correspondents.

539.   Williams, Herbert L. **The Newspaperman's President: Harry S. Truman**. Chicago: Nelson-Hall, 1984. 243 p. notes.

This journalistic but thorough study of Truman's relations with the press describes a president with a distinctive personal style that came through clearly in his communications with the media.

See also Cornwell, *Presidential Leadership of Public Opinion* (entry 24); Pollard, *The Presidents and the Press* (entry 36); and Salinger, *With Kennedy* (entry 40).

6

Public Relations in American Politics

The transformation of American political campaigns in the latter half of this century has attracted much attention and scholarly research over the past twenty years. The activity of public relations specialists in this field, noted by Alice Norton in 1970 as a growing area of practice, has expanded greatly since that date in both scope and visibility. In this chapter, the first section presents works on the phenomenon of the political consultant and its effects on political campaigns. The second section treats another aspect of the public relations presence in elections: the use of communications technology (primarily television and polling techniques) in campaigns. The final section is devoted to relevant works on the politics-media relationship in general.

POLITICAL CONSULTANTS
AND CAMPAIGNS

540. Agranoff, Robert. **The Management of Election Campaigns**. Boston: Holbrook Press, 1976. 481 p. notes.
      A practical guide to campaigning, set in a theoretical framework, for students and campaigners. One chapter is devoted to campaign public relations and several others deal with media use. The author is a political scientist and campaign consultant.

541. Agranoff, Robert, comp. **The New Style in Election Campaigns**. 2d ed. Boston: Holbrook Press, 1976. 471 p. notes.
      A book of readings to accompany the preceding text. One section presents selections on professional campaign management; other articles discuss uses of media, information systems, and ethical concerns.

542. American Institute for Political Communication. **The 1972 Presidential Campaign: Nixon Administration-Mass Media Relationship**. Washington, DC: AIPC, 1974. 425 p. notes.
      One in a series of in-depth studies of the Nixon administration's relationships with the media. (*See also* entry 484.)

543. Bloom, Melvyn H. **Public Relations and Presidential Campaigns: A Crisis in Democracy**. New York: Crowell, 1973. 349 p. bibliography.
      A study by a political scientist/journalist of public relations involvement in campaigns from 1952 to 1972, documenting the increasing dominance of political consultants.

544. Blumenthal, Sidney. **The Permanent Campaign: Inside the World of Elite Political Operatives**. Boston: Beacon, 1980. 264 p.
      Profiles of many of the best-known political consultants, plus a few candidates, showing how they mount their campaigns.

545. Chagall, David. **The New Kingmakers**. New York: Harcourt Brace Jovanovich, 1981. 419 p.

The author examines the role of campaign consultants with special reference to the Nixon, Carter, and Reagan election campaigns. The work is written in a popular style and the author is neutral regarding current campaign practices.

546. Crouse, Timothy. **The Boys on the Bus**. New York: Random House, 1972. 383 p.

Based on an article in *Rolling Stone*, this work offers the journalist's view of candidates' press conferences and other political campaign events.

547. Gold, Vic. **PR as in President**. Garden City, NY: Doubleday, 1977. 251 p.

Impressions of the 1976 presidential campaign by a retired public relations consultant.

548. Hiebert, Ray E., et al., eds. **The Political Image Merchants: Strategies for the Seventies**. Washington, DC: Acropolis, 1975. 302 p. notes.

Essays of varying length, most by practicing political consultants, from a 1971 seminar. Topics covered include new campaign techniques, uses of television, polls and surveys, direct mail, and applications of computer technology. Ethical questions are also considered.

549. Jamieson, Kathleen H. **Packaging the Presidency: A History and Criticism of Presidential Campaign Advertising**. New York: Oxford, 1984. 505 p. notes. bibliography.

A study of advertising strategies, particularly on television, in presidential campaigns from 1952 through 1980.

550. Leary, Mary Ellen. **Phantom Politics: Campaigning in California**. Washington, DC: Public Affairs Press, 1977. 191 p.

A research study of the 1974 election of Jerry Brown, described as a television-oriented and intentionally issueless campaign in which the media allowed themselves to be manipulated into limiting opportunities for public involvement.

551. Mauser, Gary A. **Political Marketing: An Approach to Campaign Strategy**. New York: Praeger, 1983. 304 p. bibliography.

An application of marketing concepts to campaigning, written for both campaign managers and academic audiences. Marketing theory and research on new product development and positioning are applied to California and French election campaigns.

552. Napolitan, Joseph. **The Election Game and How to Win It**. New York: Doubleday, 1972. 300 p.

Personal experiences of a well-known political consultant who describes himself as a "specialist in political communication".

553. Nimmo, Dan D. **The Political Persuaders: The Techniques of Modern Election Campaigns**. Englewood Cliffs, NJ: Prentice-Hall, 1970. 214 p. notes.

Nimmo was one of the early observers of the phenomenon of political parties being supplanted by professional campaign managers. In this study of modern campaign technology, he also documents the replacement of issues by images in campaigns.

554. Nimmo, Dan D., and Savage, Robert. **Candidates and Their Images: Concepts, Methods and Findings**. Pacific Palisades, CA: Goodyear, 1976. 250 p. notes.

The authors examine various aspects of candidates' images: determinants, styles, effects of public exposure, and impact on voter behavior. A comprehensive treatment of the subject with a review of the literature.

555. Sabato, Larry J. **The Rise of Political Consultants: New Ways of Winning Elections**. New York: Basic, 1981. 376 p. notes. bibliographic essay.

Based on interviews with political consultants, this study describes the new campaign techniques of polling, television advertising, and direct mailing. The author also discusses ethical problems in current campaign practices and the American Association of Political Consultants' attempt to develop a code of ethics.

556. Vermeer, Jan P. **For Immediage Release: Candidate Press Releases in American Political Campaigns**. Westport, CT: Greenwood, 1982. 189 p. notes. bibliography.

A research study on the effectiveness of the press release in campaigns.

557. Zisk, Betty H. **Money, Media, and the Grass Roots: State Ballot Issues and the Electoral Process**. Sage Library of Social Research, vol. 164. Newbury Park, CA: Sage, 1987. 279 p. notes. bibliography.

A study of spending, media coverage, and voting behavior in the campaigns for initiatives and referenda, constitutional amendments, and bond issues in four states between 1976 and 1982. Strategies employed by businesses, political consultants, and grass-roots organizations are examined. Among the author's findings: heavy spending led to victory in 78 percent of the cases.

See also Kaid and Wadsworth, *Political Campaign Communication* (entry 273); Kelley, *Professional Public Relations and Political Power* (entry 28); McGinniss, *The Selling of the President, 1968* (entry 31); Newman and Sheth, *Political Marketing* (entry 276); and Perry, *The New Politics* (entry 34).

POLITICAL USES OF NEW TECHNOLOGY

Useful subject headings relating to this topic include Mass media--Political aspects, Television in politics, and Advertising, political.

558. Altschuler, Bruce E. **Keeping a Finger on the Public Pulse: Private Polling and Presidential Elections**. Westport, CT: Greenwood, 1982. 197 p. notes. bibliography.

A general examination of the use of polls to measure public opinion in political campaigns. Relevant to the study of public relations because of the important role polling now plays in both political and nonpolitical settings.

559. Barber, James D., ed. **Race for the Presidency: The Media and the Nominating Process**. Englewood Cliffs, NJ: Prentice-Hall for the American Assembly, 1978. 205 p.

Essays on candidates' media strategies, especially during the early campaigns of the presidential candidates in the 1976 election.

560. Blume, Keith. **The Presidential Election Show: Campaign 84 and Beyond on the Nightly News**. South Hadley, MA: Bergin & Garvey, 1985. 340 p. bibliography.

An examination of the role of television in the Mondale-Reagan campaign. The author, a producer of television documentaries, is critical of the quality of political journalism on television.

561. Diamond, Edwin, and Bates, Stephen. **The Spot: The Rise of Political Advertising on Television**. Cambridge, MA: MIT Press, 1984. 416 p. notes.

Through a study of political advertising on television ("polispots") from 1952 to 1980 and through interviews with leading media managers, the authors identify positive and negative effects of television on the political campaign process.

562. Gilbert, Robert E. **Television and Presidential Politics**. North Quincy, MA: Christopher Publishing House, 1972. 335 p. bibliography.

From an analysis of presidential campaigns between 1952 and 1968, the author notes the nationalizing effect of television in politics, the increased costs of campaigning, and the enhanced power of the president.

563. Lang, Gladys E., and Lang, Kurt. **Politics and Television Re-viewed**. Newbury Park, CA: Sage, 1984. 223 p. notes.

Continuing the authors' study of television and its effects (*Politics and Television*, Chicago: Quadrangle, 1968) this work examines live coverage of political events and attempts to determine how the televising of such events affects viewers' political behavior.

564. Linsky, Martin, ed. **Television and the Presidential Elections: Self-Interest and the Public Interest**. Lexington, MA: Lexington, 1983. 137 p. bibliography.

A collection of papers examining television involvement in presidential campaigns, based on a conference of journalists, media executives, lawyers, and political scientists.

565. Martel, Myles. **Political Campaign Debates: Images, Strategies and Tactics**. White Plains, NY: Longman, 1983. 193 p. notes. bibliography.

The author, debate advisor for Ronald Reagan, discusses the importance of image and describes debate preparation tactics and strategies, verbal and nonverbal.

566. Mickelson, Sig. **The Electric Mirror: Politics in an Age of Television**. New York: Dodd, Mead, 1972. 304 p. notes. bibliography.

The author describes political uses of television up to the early 1970s, not only in the United States but also in Europe and Japan.

567. Minow, Newton N.; Martin, John B.; and Mitchell, Lee M. **Presidential Television**. New York: Basic, 1973. 232 p. notes.

From an examination of Nixon's use of television while president, the authors proceed to a consideration of problems of unequal candidate and party access to the television medium and suggestions for reforms.

568. Patterson, Thomas E. **The Mass Media Election: How Americans Choose Their President.** New York: Praeger, 1980. 203 p. notes. bibliography.

A research study by a political scientist on determinants of voter behavior, using a panel survey with multiple interviews of participants over the course of the 1976 presidential campaign. The shift from a political to a stylistic presentation of candidates' images in the media is noted.

569. Patterson, Thomas E., and McClure, Robert D. **The Unseeing Eye: The Myth of Television Power in National Politics.** New York: Putnam, 1976. 218 p. notes.

After studying the manipulative and informative content of television, the authors conclude that television is not as influential in politics as had been thought; it is apparently most effective in presenting issues.

570. Ranney, Austin. **Channels of Power: The Impact of Television on American Politics.** New York: Basic for The American Enterprise Institute, 1983. 207 p. notes.

A study of the effects of television on political campaigns and political activities in general.

571. Saldich, Anne R. **Electronic Democracy: Television's Impact on the American Political Process.** New York: Praeger, 1979. 122 p. bibliography.

The aim of this work is to inform the public about television's political effects so that better quality information will be demanded. Topics include the use of television by presidents and government propaganda.

572. Schram, Martin. **The Great American Video Game: Presidential Politics in the Television Age.** New York: Morrow, 1987. 328 p.

An examination of television news reporting of the 1984 presidential campaign, with the author concluding that television gives the public what the politicians want them to see and what is good for the ratings.

573. Spero, Robert. **The Duping of the American Voter: Dishonesty and Deception in Presidential Television Advertising.** New York: Lippincott & Crowell, 1980. 232 p. bibliography.

A study of political advertising from 1952 to 1976, emphasizing its negative aspects and suggesting possible options for reform.

574. Wilhelmsen, Frederick D., and Bret, Jane. **Telepolitics: The Politics of Neuronic Man.** Plattsburgh, NY: Tundra Books, 1972. 254 p. bibliography.

A position statement on how television has transformed politics into government by personality, with the real power in the hands of behind-the-scenes experts.

See also MacNeil, *The People Machine* (entry 30); and Wyckoff, *The Image Candidates* (entry 43).

OTHER ASPECTS OF THE POLITICS-MEDIA RELATIONSHIP

The titles listed here provide other perspectives on the relationships between the media and political activity. Their relevance to public relations consists, for the most part, of supplying background information or a context for understanding political public relations functions.

575. Arterton, F. Christopher. **Media Politics: The News Strategies of Presidential Campaigns**. Lexington, MA: Heath, 1984. 220 p. notes.
    A scholarly study, based on the 1976 and 1980 presidential campaigns, of the effects of news reporting on campaign conduct, suggesting ways in which political journalism can be improved.

576. Gandy, Oscar H., Jr. **Beyond Agenda Setting: Information Subsidies and Public Policy**. Norwood, NJ: Ablex, 1982. 243 p. notes. bibliography.
    Using an economic framework, the author examines policy makers' uses of information subsidies. Public relations practitioners are described as major technicians in the agenda-setting process; the practices and motives of government public information officers are also explored. A survey of the research literature on media content and influence is included.

577. Gans, Herbert J. **Deciding What's News: A Study of CBS Evening News, NBC Nightly News, Newsweek and Time**. New York: Pantheon, 1979. 393 p. bibliography.
    An examination of social, historical, and political influences on news reporting. The author, a sociologist, considers political power, "reality judgments," and journalistic values as major factors in determining how journalists select and present the news.

578. Graber, Doris A. **Processing the News: How People Tame the Information Tide**. White Plains, NY: Longman, 1984. 241 p. notes. bibliography.
    A study, based on a year-long research project, of the effects of political communication on the recipients: specifically, how people use the news in forming opinions.

579. MacKuen, Michael B., and Coombs, Steven L. **More Than News: Media Power in Public Affairs**. Newbury Park, CA: Sage, 1981. 231 p. bibliographies.
    Two studies based on dissertations; the authors conclude that the media do influence public opinion and actions but not excessively.

580. Rubin, Richard L. **Press, Party and Presidency**. New York: Norton, 1981. 246 p. notes.
    A description of changes in political processes and relationships resulting from the evolution of the media. Among the effects noted are the growing centralization of the press, the greater role of primaries, and the decrease in influence of political parties.

7
Public Relations in Nonprofit Organizations

Because nonprofit organizations depend on public goodwill for funding, workers, and their very existence, public relations is a vital element in the management of such organizations. However, their financial resources for public relations research, planning, and program implementation are often limited. Commitment of top management and appropriate staff support for the public relations function are important prerequisites for a successful program.

Nonprofit bodies typically use public relations to attract members and funds and to publicize their cause or social contribution. Their publics include potential and actual volunteers and donors, members, clients, staff, foundations and government agencies, legislators, community groups, related organizations, and the general public. Many of the communication techniques and activities of public relations practitioners in nonprofit bodies are similar to those of other organizations. A few, such as public service advertising and fund raising planning, assume greater importance in nonprofit public relations.

In this chapter, works dealing with nonprofit public relations in general are listed first, followed by material describing public relations activities and needs in some of the major types of nonprofit institutions and organizations.

NONPROFIT ORGANIZATIONS IN GENERAL

581. Berry, Jeffrey M. **Lobbying for the People: the Political Behavior of Public Interest Groups**. Princeton, NJ: Princeton University Press, 1977. 331 p. bibliography.

A research study of public interest group lobbying, focusing on the decision making process and lobbying tactics.

582. Broce, Thomas E. **Fund Raising: The Guide to Raising Money from Private Sources**. 2d ed. Norman, OK: University of Oklahoma Press, 1986. 290 p. bibliography.

Written for educational and other nonprofit institutions, this guidebook covers annual campaigns, foundation giving, corporate philanthropy, organizing for fund raising, and the role of boards and development committees. First edition published in 1979.

583. Institute for Public Relations Research and Education. **Managing Your Public Relations: Guidelines for Nonprofit Organizations**. 6 vols. New York: Institute for Public Relations Research and Education, 1977.

A set of short guidebooks on the following topics: planning, using publicity, working with volunteers, setting standards, evaluating results, and managing special events.

584. Gaby, Patricia V., and Gaby, Daniel M. **Nonprofit Organization Handbook: A Guide to Fund Raising, Grants, Lobbying, Membership Building, Publicity and Public Relations**. Englewood Cliffs, NJ: Prentice-Hall, 1979. 333 p. bibliography.

A practical guide with examples in a loose-leaf format. The writing style is informal and prescriptive. Topics covered, in addition to those named in the title, include communicating with members and staff and handling meetings and conferences.

585. Goldenberg, Edie N. **Making the Papers: The Access of Resource-Poor Groups to the Metropolitan Press**. Lexington, MA: Heath, 1975. 164 p. notes. bibliography.

A research study of the dynamics of a particular public relations problem, focusing on specific group and media characteristics and situational factors. The author concludes that for the resource-poor (typically, groups that lack status, official standing, information, knowledge, and money), media access is difficult. Some specific factors that can facilitate access by these groups are identified.

586. Hirsch, Glenn, and Lewis, Alan. **Strategies for Access to Public Service Advertising**. San Francisco, CA: Public Media Center, 1976. 63 p.

A guide to the preparation of public service announcements (PSAs) for social-change agencies. The Public Media Center is a nonprofit agency that prepares PSAs for other organizations. The text urges the use of this media-access strategy to counteract the power of corporate advertising and describes the intent and applications of the Fairness Doctrine.

587. Kipps, Harriett C., ed. **Community Resources Directory**. 2d ed. Detroit, MI: Gale, 1984. 943 p.

A directory of organizations and their publications prepared for the use of the volunteer community. Included are national resource groups, training programs, and information on local volunteer programs. Although the arrangement of entries is confusing, this directory contains useful resources for public relations and fund raising activities.

588. Leibert, Edwin R., and Sheldon, Bernice E. **Handbook of Special Events for Nonprofit Organizations: Tested Ideas for Fund Raising and Public Relations**. New York: Association Press, 1972. 224 p. bibliography.

Practical guidelines for a variety of special events, with case studies and experience reports from the field and the media.

589. Maddalena, Lucille A. **A Communications Manual for Nonprofit Organizations**. New York: Amacom, 1981. 222 p. bibliography.

Topics include speakers' bureau, meetings, advertising, publications, media relations, and two-way communication.

590. Ornstein, Norman J., and Elder, Shirley. **Interest Groups, Lobbying, and Policymaking**. Washington, DC: CQ Press, 1978. 245 p. bibliography.

The authors describe how interest groups operate, including a chapter on their resources and strategies; includes three case studies.

591. Rice, Ronald E., and Paisley, William J., eds. **Public Communication Campaigns**. Newbury Park, CA: Sage, 1981. 328 p. bibliography.

Contributions from a conference (devoted to wildfire prevention) on the topic of making communication effective in campaigns that seek to educate the public on general-welfare issues. Includes an extensive bibliography.

592. Ruffner, Robert H. **Handbook of Publicity and Public Relations for the Nonprofit Organization**. Englewood Cliffs, NJ: Prentice-Hall, 1984. 247 p. notes.

A comprehensive examination of the contemporary nonprofit organization and the techniques and tools of its public relations activities. The author stresses that careful study of its environment and planning its role in the community are critical activities for the nonprofit entity. Public relations is viewed as a two-way communication process and an integral part of the organization's management.

593. Yarrington, Roger. **Community Relations Handbook**. Longman Series in Public Communication. White Plains, NY: Longman, 1983. 236 p. notes.

A basic work for beginners in community-service organizations; communications techniques are emphasized. The textbook format includes problems, exercises, and additional readings for each chapter.

ARTS ORGANIZATIONS

594. Brownrigg, W. Grant. **Corporate Fund Raising: A Practical Plan of Action**. New York: American Council for the Arts, 1978. 72 p.

A short, practical sequence of topics—developing essential documents, strategy, and scope of the fund drive, and more—with examples.

595. Brownrigg, W. Grant. *Effective Corporate Fundraising*. New York: American Council for the Arts, 1982. 161 p.

A practical book of advice for arts organizations' fund raising campaigns, including a description of the business market and arguments for business support.

596. Melillo, Joseph V., ed. **Market the Arts!** New York: Foundation for the Extension and Development of the American Professional Theatre, 1983. 287 p. bibliography.

Application of marketing concepts to theater, dance, opera, and other performing arts. The appendices present representative marketing campaigns, a planning outline, and a list of organizations.

CHARITIES

597. Bakal, Carl. **Charity USA: An Investigation into the Hidden World of the Multibillion Dollar Charity Industry**. New York: Times Books, 1979. 498 p. notes.

A popular survey of the charity industry, including its donors, recipients, fund raising techniques, and campaign examples.

CHURCHES

598. DeVries, Charles, ed. **Religious Public Relations Handbook: For Local Congregations of All Denominations**. 3d ed. New York: Religious Public Relations Council, 1982. 56 p. bibliography.

A practical guide to public relations planning and implementation techniques. The bibliography emphasizes low-cost resources for producing print and nonprint materials.

599. Sumrall, Velma, and Germany, Lucille. **Telling the Story of the Local Church: The Who, What, When, Where, and Why of Communication**. New York: Seabury, 1979. 117 p.

The authors deal with internal and external communication. Appendix material includes information on radio and television associations and publications, cassette tapes, and types of print communications.

EDUCATIONAL INSTITUTIONS

600. Bloland, Harland G. **Associations in Action: The Washington, D.C. Higher Education Community**. ASHE-ERIC Higher Education Report no. 2. Washington, DC: George Washington University/Association for the Study of Higher Education, 1985. 116 p. bibliography.

A study of the major higher education associations and their political activities over the past twenty-five years. A comprehensive literature survey is included.

601. Bronzan, Robert T. **Public Relations, Promotions and Fund-Raising for Athletic and Physical Education Programs**. New York: Wiley, 1977. 268 p. bibliography.

Written for directors of school and college athletic programs and other educational administrators, this book presents the steps in planning and implementing public relations programs and provides examples of successful programs. Fund raising techniques and programs are also described. Checklists for planning different types of programs are included in the appendix.

602. Dunn, John A., Jr. **Enhancing the Management of Fund Raising**. New Directions for Institutional Research, no. 51. San Francisco, CA: Jossey-Bass, 1986. 100 p. notes.

A guide to planning a fund raising campaign for higher education administrators, with a summary of research and work in progress.

603. Hilldrup, Robert P. **Improving School Public Relations**. Newton, MA: Allyn & Bacon, 1982. 225 p. notes.

Practical techniques from a school superintendent, written in an informal style.

604. Jones, J. William. **Building Public Confidence for Your Schools: A Source Book of Proven PR Practices**. Arlington, VA: National School Public Relations Association, 1978. 224 p. bibliography.

A basic guide for school personnel, presenting ideas for effective communication programs.

605. Kindred, Leslie W.; Bagin, Don; and Gallagher, Donald R. **The School and Community Relations**. 3d ed. Englewood Cliffs, NJ: Prentice-Hall, 1984. 339 p.

A general text on the subject, with lists of suggested readings after each chapter.

606. Kobre, Sidney. **Successful Public Relations for Colleges and Universities**. New York: Hastings, 1974. 452 p. bibliography.

An introduction to public relations for four-year and two-year colleges, including publications, advertising, media use, special events, alumni relations, and program evaluation.

607.   Kotler, Philip, and Fox, Karen F. A. **Strategic Marketing for Educational Institutions.** Englewood Cliffs, NJ: Prentice-Hall, 1985. 396 p. notes.

A textbook that applies basic marketing elements and activities to higher education to attract both students and donors.

608.   Rowland, A. Westley, ed. **Handbook of Institutional Advancement.** 2d ed. San Francisco, CA: Jossey-Bass for the Council for Advancement and Support of Education, 1986. 796 p. notes. bibliographic essays.

A substantial general reference work on the subject of educational and institutional development. Some of the chapters include bibliographic essays.

609.   Rowland, A. Westley, ed. **New Directions for Institutional Advancement** (series). San Francisco, CA: Jossey-Bass, 1978-1982.

A series of monographs on higher education public relations topics, each with its own title and editor.

No. 1.   Jacobson, Harvey K., ed. *Evaluating Advancement Programs.* 1978. 117 p. bibliography.

No. 2.   Goldhaber, Gerald M., ed. *Improving Institutional Communication.* 1978. 99 p. bibliography.

No. 3.   Heemann, Warren, ed. *Analyzing the Cost Effectiveness of Fund Raising.* 1979. 91 p. notes.

No. 4.   Williams, Dorothy F., ed. *Communicating with Alumni.* 1979. 120 p. notes.

No. 5.   Ciervo, Arthur V., ed. *Using the Mass Media.* 1979. 97 p. notes.

No. 6.   Francis, J. Bruce, ed. *Surveying Institutional Constituencies.* 1979. 100 p. notes.

No. 7.   Welch, Patrice A., ed. *Increasing Annual Giving.* 1980. 112 p. bibliography.

No. 8.   Fisher, James L., ed. *Presidential Leadership in Advancement Activities.* 1980. 98 p. notes.

No. 9.   Maddalena, Lucille A., ed. *Encouraging Voluntarism and Volunteers.* 1980. 95 p. notes.

No. 10.   Rowland, Howard R., ed. *Effective Community Relations.* 1980. 120 p. bibliography.

No. 11.   Ross, J. David, ed. *Understanding and Increasing Foundation Support.* 1981. 94 p. bibliography.

No. 12.   Johnson, Marvin D., ed. *Successful Governmental Relations.* 1981. 97 p. notes.

No. 13.   Willmer, Wesley K., ed. *Advancing the Small College.* 1981. 119 p. notes.

No. 14. Frantzreb, Arthur C., ed. *Trustee's Role in Advancement*. 1981. 103 p. notes.

No. 15. Bryant, Peter S., and Johnson, Jane A., eds. *Advancing the Two-Year College*. 1982. 113 p. notes.

No. 16. Hobbs, Walter C., ed. *Understanding Academic Law*. 1982. 94 p. notes.

610. Unruh, Adolph, and Willier, Robert A. **Public Relations for Schools**. Belmont, CA: Fearon, 1974. 169 p. bibliography.

An introduction to public school public relations, for use by educators, community leaders, and as a higher education textbook.

611. Walling, Donovan R. **Complete Book of School Public Relations: An Administrator's Manual and Guide**. Englewood Cliffs, NJ: Prentice-Hall, 1982. 222 p. notes.

Practical techniques for communicating with many of the school's publics: taxpayers, parents, community and political groups, unions, and teachers.

612. West, Philip T. **Educational Public Relations**. Newbury Park, CA: Sage, 1985. 288 p. notes.

A text for educators with case studies.

613. Willmer, Wesley K. **The Small College Advancement Program: Managing for Results**. Washington, DC: Council for Advancement and Support of Education, 1981. 145 p. notes. bibliography.

A study, based on the author's dissertation, of a range of advancement activities in small independent colleges, including alumni programs, fund raising, publications, recruitment, and institutional relations.

See also Constantine, *An Annotated and Extended Bibliography of Higher Education Marketing* (entry 268), and Ryans and Shanklin, *Strategic Planning, Marketing and Public Relations, and Fund-Raising in Higher Education* (entry 279).

HEALTH-CARE ORGANIZATIONS

614. American Society for Hospital Marketing and Public Relations. **Basic Guide to Hospital Public Relations**. 2d ed. Chicago: American Hospital Publishing Co., 1984. 96 p. notes. bibliography.

A basic overview in which public relations, defined as goal-oriented communication, is described in terms of its communication programs and its management aspects.

615. Bachner, John P. **Public Relations for Nursing Homes**. Springfield, IL: Charles C. Thomas, 1974. 159 p.

The author defines public relations in terms of practical tools and techniques used to communicate to publics. Short chapters outline these skills and describe the nursing home's publics.

616.   Bagwell, Marilyn, and Clements, Sallee. **A Political Handbook for Health Professionals**. Boston: Little, Brown, 1985. 308 p. bibliography.

This volume covers lobbying, communicating with legislators, negotiating, party activity, PACs, and media exposure; also, a section on power and the legislative process. The need for unified action is emphasized. Appendices provide lists of national and state political resources and professional organizations.

617.   Brennan, Jim. **Public Relations Can Be Fun and Easy, Especially for Nursing Home People**. Continuing Education for Health Care Providers. Mt. Kisco, NY: Futura, 1977. 337 p. bibliography.

In short chapters, using illustrations and examples, the author covers the organization of the public relations function and its major activities.

618.   Hogan, Norma S. **Humanizing Health Care: The Task of the Patient Representative**. Oradell, NJ: Medical Economics, 1980. 190 p. notes.

The author is founder of the American Hospital Association's Society of Patient Representatives. This linking function between patient and institution is thoroughly described with historical background, models,. functions, and relationship to risk management.

619.   Kreps, Gary C., and Thornton, Barbara C. **Health Communication: Theory and Practice**. White Plains, NY: Longman, 1984. 287 p. notes. bibliography.

This work is intended as an interdisciplinary textbook for health and social-work professionals and administrators. Includes selected readings. Its coverage includes oral, written, and organizational communication; media; client-practitioner relationships and group-practice problems; and intercultural and ethical considerations. An extensive bibliography (forty-two pages) supplements the chapter notes.

620.   McMillan, Norman H. **Marketing Your Hospital: A Strategy for Survival**. Chicago: American Hospital Association, 1981. 117 p. bibliography.

Public relations is viewed as an aspect of marketing in this practical guide to marketing planning and implementation. The author is a marketing executive and hospital trustee.

621.   Riggs, Lew, ed. **The Health Care Facility's Public Relations Handbook**. Rockville, MD: Aspen Systems, 1982. 253 p. notes.

Experts in medical and health-care public relations have contributed chapters on the full range of public relations management and communication functions.

LABOR ORGANIZATIONS

622.   Douglas, Sara U. **Labor's New Voice: Unions and the Mass Media**. Norwood, NJ: Ablex, 1986. 310 p. bibliography.

Examines the use of mass media by unions, specifically in union attempts to organize workers in a company.

LIBRARIES

623. Angoff, Allan, ed. **Public Relations for Libraries: Essays in Communications Techniques**. Westport, CT: Greenwood, 1973. 246 p. notes.
Public relations for different types of libraries, including an essay by Bernays. Many of the contributors describe their own experiences.

624. Edsall, Marian S. **Library Promotion Handbook**. Phoenix, AZ: Oryx, 1980. 244 p. bibliography.
A practical guide with a public library focus, including many examples.

625. Edsall, Marian S. **Practical PR for School Library Media Centers**. New York: Neal-Schuman, 1984. 165 p. bibliography.
A practical guide covering promotional and publicity activities, emphasizing raising awareness and developing a favorable image of the media center.

626. Kies, Cosette N. **Marketing and Public Relations for Libraries**. Metuchen, NJ: Scarecrow, 1987. 202 p. notes. bibliography.
Viewing public relations as an administrative tool, the author presents a two-way communication model and provides a history of library public relations, discussion of theoretical concepts, practical techniques, and current trends. The bibliography is short but well-chosen.

627. Rice, Betty. **Public Relations for Public Libraries: Creative Problem Solving**. New York: Wilson, 1972. 133 p. bibliography.
Although it is somewhat out-of-date in its treatment of media, this work provides an introduction to public library public relations, including a section on managing bond and budget campaigns.

628. Rummel, Kathleen K., and Perica, Esther, eds. **Persuasive Public Relations for Libraries**. Chicago: American Library Association, LAMA Publications Section, 1983. 199 p. bibliography.
Public relations in a marketing context for all types of libraries. Includes information on special ALA resources available and an extensive bibliography.

629. Underwood, Bob. **The Visible Library: Practical Public Relations for Public Librarians**. London: Library Association, 1981. 207 p. bibliography.
A British overview of the purposes, methods, and publics of public relations. The author uses examples from Great Britain and the United States.

630. Weingand, Darlene E., ed. **Marketing for Libraries and Information Agencies**. Norwood, NJ: Ablex, 1984. 130 p. notes.
Marketing theory applied to libraries of all types.

MUSEUMS

631.   Adams, G. Donald. **Museum Public Relations**. AASLH Management Series, vol. 2. Nashville, TN: American Associations for State and Local History, 1983. 237 p. notes. bibliography.

A comprehensive handbook for museums with small and large budgets, covering planning and research, identification of publics, fund raising techniques, publications, use of media, promotional campaigns, and public relations in daily operations. Both print and visual examples are included.

SOCIAL-WELFARE ORGANIZATIONS

632.   Brawley, Edward A. **Mass Media and Human Services: Getting the Message Across**. Newbury Park, CA: Sage, 1983. 240 p. notes.

Written for social workers, this guide shows how to use the media to inform and educate the public. Useful references are provided with each chapter.

633.   Nelson, Roberta. **Creating Community Acceptance for Handicapped People**. Springfield, IL: Charles C. Thomas, 1978. 220 p. notes. bibliography.

A guide for managing a special communication problem, with chapters on identifying barriers, planning and implementation, issues, and support organizations.

Author/Title Index

Reference is to entry number, unless otherwise indicated.

ABA Banking Journal, 247
ABI/Inform, 303
Abt, Clark C., 447
Academy of Management Journal, 222
Across the Board, 248
Adams, G. Donald, 631
Advancing Public Relations Education, 181
Advancing the Small College, 609
Advancing the Two-Year College, 609
Adversaries, The, 510
Advertising Age, 249
Advocacy Advertising and Large Corporations, 339
Agee, Warren K., 68
Agranoff, Robert, 540, 541
Alexander, Herbert E., 417, 418
All TV Publicity Outlets Nationwide, 144
Altheide, David L., 1
Altschuler, Bruce E., 558
Always Live Better Than Your Clients, 77
American Business Communication
    Association, 266, 272
American Institute for Political
    Communication, 233, 484, 542
American Institute of Certified Public
    Accountants, 448, 464
American Journal of Sociology, 237
American Management Association, 322
American Political Science Association,
    229, 291
American Political Science Review, 229
American Politics Quarterly, 230
American President, The, 532
American Society for Hospital Marketing
    and Public Relations, 614
American Society of Association
    Executives, 261
America's Third Revolution, 408
*Analyzing the Cost Effectiveness
    of Fund Raising*, 609

Andriole, Stephen J., 343
Angoff, Allan, 623
*Annotated and Extended Bibliography
    of Higher Education Marketing,
    An*, 268
*Annual Survey of Corporate Contribu-
    tions*, 425
Anshen, Melvin, 434, 435
Anson, Edward M., 89
Aram, John D., 44
Armstrong, William G., Jr., 382
Arnold, David S., 477
Aronoff, Craig E., 45, 391
Arterton, F. Christopher, 575
Arts and Humanities Citation Index,
    285
Arts and Humanities Search, 305
Asher, Spring, 99
Ashley, Paul P., 90
Assault on the Media, 531
Association and Society Manager, 260
Association for Business Communication,
    217
Association for Education in Journalism,
    181, 182
Association for Education in Journalism
    and Mass Communication, 220,
    221, 295, 296
Association Management, 261
Association Trends, 262
Associations in Action, 600
Attack on Corporate America, The,
    351
Ault, Philip H., 68
A-V Online, 304
    print version, 298
Awad, Joseph F., 2
*Ayer Public Relations and Publicity
    Style Book*, 133

Bachner, John P., 615
Bacon's International Publicity Checker, 145
Bacon's Media Alerts, 146
Bacon's Publicity Checker, 147
Bacon's Radio/TV Directory, 148
Bagin, Don, 605
Bagwell, Marilyn, 616
Bakal, Carl, 597
Balachandran, Sarojini, 266
Balsley, Ronald D., 360
Bankrolling Ballots, 402, 403
Barber, James D., 559
Barmash, Isadore, 77
Basche, James R., Jr., 452
Basic Guide to Hospital Public Relations, 614
Baskin, Otis W., 45
Bates, Don, 108
Bates, Stephen, 561
Battle for Public Opinion, The, 527
Battle Lines, 487
Bauer, Raymond A., 449
Becker, Christine S., 477
Believable Corporation, The, 366
Benn, Alec, 91
Berenbeim, Ronald E., 459
Berkson, Larry C., 485
Bernays, Edward L., 3, 20, 21, 92, 186, 274
Bernstein, Alan B., 93
Berry, Jeffrey M., 581
Best, Arthur, 359
Beyond Agenda Setting, 576
Bibliographic Index, 285
online version, 306
Bibliography for Public Relations Professionals, 278
Big Business and Presidential Power from FDR to Reagan, 73
Big Business Blunders, 462
Biography of an Idea, 20
Birsner, E. Patricia, 360
Bishop, Robert L., 267
Bivens, Thomas, 94
Black, Sam, 4, 95
Blake, David H., 450, 454
Blake, Reed H., 84

Blanchard, Robert O., 486
Blohowiak, Donald W., 392
Bloland, Harland G., 600
Bloom, Melvyn H., 543
Bloomenthal, Howard, 96
Blume, Keith, 560
Blumenthal, Sidney, 544
Blyskal, Jeff, 5
Blyskal, Marie, 5
Boddewyn, Jean J., 455, 457
Bogart, Leo, 69
Bohl, Don L., 361
Boorstin, Daniel J., 22
Boys on the Bus, The, 546
Braam, Geert P. A., 398
Bradshaw, Thornton, 436
Braestrup, Peter, 487
Brasch, Walter M., 488
Brawley, Edward A., 632
Brennan, Jim, 617
Bret, Jane, 574
Broadcasting, 240
Broadcasting/Cablecasting Yearbook, 149
Broce, Thomas E., 582
Brody, E. W., 97, 98, 365
Bronzan, Robert T., 601
Broom, Glen M., 48
Brown, James K., 340, 341, 378
Brownrigg, W. Grant, 594, 595
Bryant, Peter S., 609
Buchholz, Rogene A., 407, 437
Budd, John F., Jr., 335
Building Public Confidence for Your Schools, 604
Bureaucratic Propaganda, 1
Burger, Chester, 6
Burrelle's Media Directories, 150
Business and Society Review, 223
Business and the Development of Ghetto Enterprise, 378
Business and the Media, 391
Business Beat, The, 396
Business Environment and Public Policy, 437
Business, Government and the Public, 410
Business In Politics, 420
Business Index, 287

Business International, 455
Business Lobbies, 414
Business Marketing, 250
Business, Media and the Law, 382
Business-Media Relationship, The, 394
Business of Public Relations, The, 97
Business Periodicals Index, 288
Business Periodicals Index (online), 307
Business Representatives in Washington, The, 23
Business Roundtable, 389
Business Strategy for the Political Arena, 409
Business Week, 251
BusinessWire, 308

Cable TV Publicity Outlets Nationwide, 151
Cahill, Martin F., 457
California Management Review, 224
Candidates and Their Images, 554
Cantor, Bill, 6
Capitol Press Corps, The, 507
Carrell, Bob, 56
Carroll, Archie B., 438
Carter, David E., 330
Case for PACs, The, 417
Center, Allen H., 46, 48
Chafee, Steven H., 470
Chagall, David, 545
Chamberlain, Neil W., 439
Chambers, Wicke, 99
Channels of Communications, 241
Channels of Power, 570
Charity USA, 597
Chase, Harold W., 40
Chase, W. Howard, 346
Cheney, George, 86
Cherington, Paul W., 23
Chilling Effect in TV News, The, 528
Chittick, William O., 489
Cialdini, Robert B., 7
Ciervo, Arthur V., 609
Cigler, Allan J., 399
Clearing the Air, 82
Clements, Sallee, 616
Close to the Customer, 361

Cohn, Jules, 440
Cole, George, 100
Cole, Robert S., 187
Columbia Journalism Review, 242
Columbia University, Graduate School of Business, 323
Combs, James E., 472
Coming to Grips with Crisis, 356
Commission on Public Relations Education, 181, 182
Communicating for Productivity, 367
Communicating for Survival, 365
Communicating When Your Company Is under Siege, 357
Communicating with Alumni, 609
Communication: A Guide to Information Sources, 271
Communication Abstracts, 289
Communication by Objectives, 121
Communication Research, 213
Communication Research Associates, 200, 203, 211, 212
Communication Skills in the Organization, 51
Communication World, 193
Communications and Society, 280
Communications Manual for Nonprofit Organizations, 589
Community Relations Handbook, 593
Community Resources Directory, 587
Company Image, The, p. 58
Competing for Capital in the '80s, 374
Complete Book of School Public Relations, 611
Conference Board, 324
Confessions of a PR Man, 83
Confidence Gap, The, 13
Confirm or Deny, 495
Congress and the News Media, 486
Conscience of the Corporations, The, 440
Constantine, Karen K., 268
Consumer Affairs Department, The, 363
Consumer Input for Marketing Decisions, 362
Controversy Advertising, 341
Coombs, Steven L., 579
Cooper, Martha R., 414

Cornwell, Elmo E., Jr., 24
Corporate Advertising, 327
Corporate Aid Programs in Twelve Less-Developed Countries, 461
Corporate Communications Report, 201
Corporate Contributions Function, The, 432
Corporate Crisis Management, 343
Corporate Economic Education Programs, 336
Corporate External Affairs, 455
Corporate 500, 180
Corporate Fund Raising, 594
Corporate Identity Design, 332
Corporate Image, The, 281
Corporate PACs and Federal Campaign Financing Laws, 421
Corporate Performance, 389
Corporate Personality, The, 333
Corporate Philanthropic Public Service Activities, 428
Corporate Public Affairs Office, The, 385
Corporate Public Issues and Their Management, 202
Corporate Public Relations: A New Historical Perspective, 74
Corporate Social Audit, The, 449
Corporate Social Reporting in the United States and Western Europe, 452
Corporate Speech Writer's Handbook, The, 140
Corporate Strategies for Social Performance, 434
Corporate Strategy, Public Policy and the Fortune 500, 407
Corporate Video in Focus, 335
Corporate Voluntary Contributions in Europe, 431
Corporations and Political Accountability, 406
Corporations and Their Critics, 436
Corrado, Frank M., 101
Corson, John J., 451
Coulson-Thomas, Colin, 102
Council for Advancement and Support of Education, 263, 608, 613
Council on Economic Priorities, 402, 403, 441

Courtier to the Crowd, 26
Crable, Richard E., 47
Crano, William D., 137
Creating Community Acceptance for Handicapped People, 633
Creation of Consent, 18
Credibility Problem, The, 484
Crisis Management: A Team Approach, 354
Crisis Management: Planning for the Inevitable, 348
Crisis of Confidence, 468
Crissy, W. J. E., 284
Critical Issues in Public Relations, 10
Crouse, Timothy, 546
Culligan, Matthew J., 103
Currah, Philip, 456
Current Index to Journals in Education, 290. *See also* ERIC
Currents, 263
Customer Education, 364
Cutlip, Scott M., 48

Dannelley, Paul, 269
Danzig, Fred, 117
D'Aprix, Roger M., 366, 367
Darnay, Brigitte T., 152
Daubert, Harold E., 104
Deakin, James, 516
Deciding What's News, 577
Defenders and Shapers of the Corporate Image, 9
Denton, Robert E., Jr., 517
Design for Public Relations Education, A, 182
Designing Corporate Identity Programs for Small Corporations, 330
Designs for Persuasive Communication, 12
Dessart, George, 105
Detz, Joan, 106
Deutsch, Arnold, 368
Developing a Corporate Identity, 136
DeVries, Charles, 598
Diamond, Edwin, 561
Diary of James C. Hagerty, The, 521
Dilenschneider, Robert L., 85

Directory of Business-Related Political Action Committees, 173
Directory of Registered Lobbyists and Lobbyist Legislation, 174
Dissertation Abstracts Online, 309
Doctoral Dissertations in Political Science in Universities of the United States, 291
Dominguez, George S., 400
Douglas, George A., 107
Douglas, Sara U., 622
Druck, Kalman B., 108, 188
Dunn, John A., Jr., 597
Dunn, S. Watson, 49, 457
Duping of the American Voter, The, 573

EC & TJ, 243
Editor and Publisher, 244
Editor and Publisher International Yearbook, 153
Edsall, Marian S., 624, 625
Educational Public Relations, 612
Educational Guide to Free Audio and Video Materials, 292
Educators Guide to Free Films, 292
Educators Guide to Free Filmstrips and Slides, 292
Eells, Richard, 426
Effective Communication, 477
Effective Community Relations, 609
Effective Corporate Fundraising, 595
Effective Public Relations, 48
Effective Publicity, 127
Effective Washington Representation, 415
Ehrenkranz, Lois B., 109
Elder, Shirley, 590
Election Game and How to Win It, The, 552
Electric Mirror, The, 566
Electronic Democracy, 571
Emanuel, Myron, 336
Emergency Public Relations Manual, 93
Employee Communication: A Bibliography, 266
Encouraging Voluntarism and Volunteers, 609

Engineering of Consent, The, 21
English, Raymond, 430
Enhancing the Management of Fund Raising, 602
Entman, Robert M., 509
Eppley, Garrett G., 478
ERIC, 310
Evaluating Advancement Programs, 609
Evans, Fred J., 393
Executive's Guide to Handling a Press Interview, The, 122
Experts in Action, 6
External Challenges to Management Decisions, 459
Ewing, Raymond P., 347

Facciola, Peter C., 297
Falcione, Raymond L., 272
Fate, Terry, 270
Fazio, James R., 479
FDR and the Press, 538
FDR's Splendid Deception, 518
Federal Government-Daily Press Relationship, The, 484
Feel of the Work Place, The, 370
Fenn, Dan H., Jr., 449
Fighting to Win, 412
Financial Analysts' Journal, 252
Financial and Economic Journalism, 373
Fine, Seymour H., 8
Fink, Steven, 348
Finn, David, 394
Firestone, O. J., 490
Fisher, James L., 609
Fiur, Merton, 108
Fixx, James F., 491
Flacks of Washington, The, 508
For Immediate Release, 556
Fornell, Claes, 362
Forrestal, Dan J., 85
Fortune, 253
Foundation for Public Relations Research and Education, *see* Institute for Public Relations Research and Education
Foundation News, 264
Fox, Karen F. A., 607

Francis, J. Bruce, 609
Frantzreb, Arthur C., 609
Fraser/Associates, 387, 419
Frederick, William C., 450
Fremont-Smith, Marion R., 427
FRM Weekly, 265
From Spokesman to Press Secretary, 534
Fry, Ronald W., 189
Fulbright, James W., 492
Fund Raising, 582
Fund Raising and Public Relations, 269
Fund-Raising, Grants and Foundations, 270
Fund Raising Management, 265
Fundamentals of Public Relations, 59
Future of Business Regulation, 411

Gaby, Daniel M., 584
Gaby, Patricia V., 584
Galambos, Louis, 70
Gale Directory of Publications, 154
Gallagher, Donald R., 605
Gallagher, Hugh G., 518
Galnoor, Itzhak, 493
Gandy, Oscar H., 576
Gans, Herbert J., 577
Garbett, Thomas F., 327
Gazette, 214
Gebbie Press All-in-One Directory, 155
Georgi, Charlotte, 270
Germany, Lucille, 599
Getting Back to the Basics of Public Relations and Publicity, 103
Getting Your Message Out, 119
Gilbert, Douglas L., 479
Gilbert, Robert E., 562
Gilbert, William H., 480
Gillen, Ralph L., 23
Gitter, A. George, 271
Going Public, 525
Gold, Vic, 547
Golden, L. L. L., 25
Goldenberg, Edie N., 585
Goldhaber, Gerald M., 609
Goldman, Jordan, 110
Gollner, Andrew B., 379

Good-bye to the Low Profile, 338
Goodsell, Charles T., 494
Gore, Chadwick R., 175
Gotcha! The Media, the Government and the Falklands Crisis, 497
Goulding, Phil G., 495
Governing the Press, 503
Government Marketing, 483
Government/Press Connection, The, 499
Government Relations, 400
Government Secrecy in Democracies, 493
Graber, Doris A., 529, 578
Graphic Artists Guild, 331
Graphic Artists Guild's Corporate and Communications Design Annual, 331
Graves, Joseph J., Jr., 371
Gray, James G., Jr., 328
Great American Video Game, The, 572
Greenbaum, Howard H., 272
Greene, Dolph, 103
Greevy, David U., 175
Grefe, Edward A., 412
Grossman, Michael B., 520
Grunig, James E., 50
Grunin, Robert, 271
Guide to Community Advocacy Skills, A, 123
Guidelines for Managing Corporate Issues Programs, 344
Gunther, Max, 83

Hagerty, James C., 521
Haggerty, Brian A., 418
Hahn, Dan F., 517
Halberstam, David, 496
Hall, Camden M., 90
Halpern, Burton M., 111
Handbook for Public Relations Writing, 94
Handbook of Advocacy Advertising, 340
Handbook of Corporate Social Responsibility, The, 380
Handbook of Institutional Advancement, 608
Handbook of Investor Relations, 375

Handbook of Organizational Communication, 86

Handbook of Political Communication, 473

Handbook of Publicity and Public Relations for the Nonprofit Organization, 587

Handbook of Special Events for Nonprofit Organizations, 588

Handbook on International Public Relations, 458

Handler, Edward, 420

Haroldsen, Edwin O., 84

Harrell, T. Allen, 125

Harris, James F., 428

Harris, Robert, 497

Harty, Sheila, 337

Harvard Business Review, 225

Harvard Business Review (online index), 311

Hayes, Michael T., 413

Health Care Facility's Public Relations Handbook, The, 621

Health Communication, 619

Heath, Robert L., 349, 350

Heemann, Warren, 609

Heise, Juergen A., 498

Hellweg, Susan A., 272

Helm, Louis M., 481

Hendrix, Jerry A., 112

Henry, Kenneth, 9

Herzstein, Robert E., 71

Hess, Stephen, 499, 500, 501

Hi-Tech Alert for the Professional Communicator, 203

Hiebert, Ray E., 26, 27, 113, 188, 211, 326, 502, 548

High Visibility, 16

Hill & Knowlton, 10, 372, 458

Hilldrup, Robert P., 603

Hirsch, Glenn, 586

Hobbs, Walter C., 609

Hogan, Norma S., 618

Holmes, Deborah, 503

How Fifteen Transnational Corporations Manage Public Affairs, 457

How to Build a Corporation's Identity and Project Its Image, 327

How to Get Publicity, 129

How to Handle Speechwriting Assignments, 122

How to Handle Your Own PR, 120

How to Prepare and Write Your Employee Handbook, 89

How to Write and Give a Speech, 106

Howard, Carole, 114

Howard, Wilfred, 115

Hucksters in the Classroom, 337

Hudson, Howard P., 116

Hudson's Newsletter Directory, 158

Hudson's Washington News Media Contacts Directory, 156

Human Communication Research, 215

Human Resources Network, 380

Human Resources Revolution, The, 368

Humanities Index, 293
   online version, 312

Humanizing Health Care, 618

Hunt, Gary T., 51

Hunt, Todd, 50

Huxford, Marilyn, 280

Ideals in Collision, 342

Image: A Guide to Pseudo-Events in America, The, 22

Image Candidates, The, 43

Image Makers, The, 275

Image Merchants, The, 39

Image, or What Happened to the American Dream, The, 22

Images and Marketing, 284

Improve Your Public Relations, 478

Improving Institutional Communication, 609

Improving School Public Relations, 603

Increasing Annual Giving, 609

Index to Journals in Communication Studies Through 1985, 297

Industrial Publicity, 104

Influence of Business Firms on the Government, 398

Influence: Science and Practice, 7

Information Establishment, The, 514

Information Today, p. 53

Information War, The, 506

Informing the People, 481
Inside Organizational Communications, 369
Inside Public Relations, 53
Institute for Public Relations Research and Education, 14, 38, 41, 85, 108, 181, 184, 185, 191, 200, 282, 583
Institute of Public Relations, 197
Institutional Investor, 254
Interest Group Politics, 399
Interest Groups, Lobbying, and Policy-making, 590
International Advertising Association, 341
International Association of Business Communicators, 130, 193, 369
International Business Philanthropy, 426
International City Management Association, 477, 480
International Communication Association, 215, 272
International Directory of Special Events and Festivals, 157
International Marketing Communications, 463
International Public Relations Association, 183, 194
International Public Relations Review, 194
Internships, Volume 1: Advertising, Marketing, Public Relations, 189
Investor Relations Handbook, 377
Investor Relations Newsletter, 204
Investor Relations That Work, 376
Investor Relations Update, 205
Investor Responsibility Research Center, 258, 259, 325
IPRA Newsletter, 194
Issue Management, 346
Issues Management, 350
It Sure Looks Different from the Inside, 529
It Was Better Than Work, 78

Jablin, Fredrick M., 86
Jack O'Dwyer's Newsletter, 206
Jacobson, Harvey K., 609
Jamieson, Kathleen H., 549
Janger, Allen R., 459

Jefkins, Frank, 52
Jenks, Stephen, 370
Jennings, Marianne M., 409
Johnson, Jane A., 609
Johnson, John M., 1
Johnson, M. Bruce, 351
Johnson, Marvin D., 609
Jones, J. William, 604
Journal of Advertising, 226
Journal of Broadcasting, 216
Journal of Broadcasting and Electronic Media, 216
Journal of Business, 294
Journal of Business Communication, 217
Journal of Communication, 218
Journal of Educational Public Relations, 195
Journal of Marketing, 227
Journal of Personality and Social Psychology, 238
Journal of Politics, 231
Journal of Social Issues, 239
Journalism Abstracts, 295
Journalism Educator, 219
Journalism Monographs, 74, 220
Journalism Quarterly, 296
Jowett, Garth S., 11
JQ: Journalism Quarterly, 296
Juergens, George, 522

Kahn, Gilbert R., 109
Kaid, Lynda L., 273, 471, 475
Kail, F. M., 504
Kalupa, Frank, 55
Kaufmann, Carl B., 408
Keeping a Finger on the Public Pulse, 558
Keeping the Corporate Image, 76
Kellar, Elizabeth K., 477
Kelley, F. Beverly, 78
Kelley, Stanley, Jr., 28
Kennedy and the Press, 40
Kennedy Crisis, The, 524
Keogh, James, 523
Kern, Montague, 524
Kernell, Samuel, 525
Kies, Cosette N., 626
Kindred, Leslie W., 605
Kipps, Harriett C., 587

Kirsch, Donald, 373
Klein, Herbert G., 526
Klein, Ted, 117
Klein, Walter J., 118
Klepper, Anne, 428
Klepper, Michael M., 119
Kobre, Sidney, 606
Koch, Frank, 429
Koenig, Fredrick, 329
Kotler, Philip, 16, 607
Kreps, Gary C., 619
Kruckeberg, Dean, 381
Kumar, Martha J., 520

Labor's New Voice, 622
Lamb, Robert, 382
Lang, Gladys E., 527, 563
Lang, Kurt, 527, 563
Larson, Keith A., 274
Lashner, Marilyn A., 528
Lasswell, Harold, 72
Later Years, The, 3
Lazer, William, 284
Leary, Mary Ellen, 550
Lefever, Ernest W., 430
Leibert, Edwin R., 588
Leonard, Margaret, 158
Lerbinger, Otto, 12, 139, 209, 352
Lerman, Allen H., 40
Lerner, Daniel, 72
Lesher, Stephan, 79
Lesly, Philip, 87, 209, 353
Lesly's Public Relations Handbook, 87
Leveraging the Impact of Public Affairs, 128
Levering, Patricia W., 524
Levering, Ralph B., 524
Levitan, Sar A., 414
Lewis, Alan, 586
Lewis, H. Gordon, 120
Library Promotion Handbook, 624
Linsky, Martin, 564
Lippmann, Walter, 29
Lipsen, Charles B., 79
Lipset, Seymour M., 13
Littlejohn, Robert F., 354
Lobbying, 281

Lobbying for the People, 581
Lobbying the Corporation, 446
Lobbyists and Legislators, 413
Londgren, Richard E., 121
Longman Dictionary of Mass Media and Communication, 88
Longman Series in Public Communication, 326
Loomis, Burdett A., 399
Lovell, Ronald P., 53
Lusterman, Seymour, 378, 383, 384, 401, 460
Lydenberg, Steven D., 402, 403, 441
Lyndon Johnson's Dual War, 537

MacDonald, J. Fred, 505
MacDougall, A. Kent, 395
MacKuen, Michael B., 579
MacNeil, Robert, 30
Maddalena, Lucille A., 589, 609
Mahon, John F., 385
Mainstream Access, Inc., 190
Making It Perfectly Clear, 526
Making the Papers, 585
Management Contents, 313
Management of Election Campaigns, The, 540
Management of Public Relations, The, 388
Managerial Competence, 383
Manager's Public Relations Handbook, The, 139
Managing Business and Public Policy, 44
Managing Business-State Government Relations, 401
Managing Corporate Contributions, 433
Managing Corporate Crises, 352
Managing Corporate External Relations, 386
Managing Corporate Political Action Committees, 422
Managing Corporate Social Responsibility, 438
Managing External Issues, 358
Managing Federal Government Relations, 401

Managing International Public Affairs, 460

Managing Investor Relations, 371

Managing Public Relations, 50

Managing the Corporate Image, 328

Managing the Corporate Social Environment, 442

Managing the External Relations of Multinational Corporations, 454

Managing the Media, 393

Managing the New Bottom Line, 347

Managing the Socially Responsible Corporation, 435

Managing Your Public Relations, 583

Marcus, Bruce W., 374

Marcuss, Stanley J., 415

Market the Arts, 596

Marketing and Public Relations for Libraries, 626

Marketing and Strategic Planning for Professional Service Firms, 469

Marketing Communications, 255

Marketing for Libraries and Information Agencies, 630

Marketing of Ideas and Social Issues, The, 8

Marketing Your Hospital, 620

Markle Foundation, 535, 536

Marston, John E., 54

Martel, Myles, 565

Martin, Dick, 122

Martin, John B., 567

Mass Comm Review, 221

Mass Media and Human Services, 632

Mass Media and Politics, The, 471

Mass Media Election, The, 568

Matasar, Ann B., 421

Mater, Jean, 482

Mathews, Wilma, 114

Matlon, Ronald J., 297

Mauksch, Mary, 431

Mauser, Gary A., 551

McClure, Robert D., 569

McCrummen, J. B., 123

McGinniss, Joe, 31

McGrath, Phyllis S., 386, 404

McGuire, E. Patrick, 363, 461

McMillan, Norman H., 620

McPhatter, William, 396

McQuaid, Kim, 73

Measurement of Corporate Social Performance, 448

Measuring Business's Social Performance, 451

Media for Managers, 101

Media Institute, The, 124

Media Politics, 575

Media Power Politics, 509

Meer, Claudia G., 364

Melillo, Joseph V., 596

Men, Women, Messages, and Media, 62

Meyers, Gerald C., 355

Mickelson, Sig, 566

Milbrath, Lester W., 32

Miles, Robert H., 442

Miles, William, 275

Mind Managers, The, 17

Minimum Disclosure, 498

Minor, Dale, 506

Minow, Newton N., 567

Mitchell, Lee M., 567

Model for Public Relations Education for Professional Practice, A, 183

Modern Public Relations, 54

Modern Talking Picture Service, 14, 292

Mokwa, Michael P., 483

Money, Media, and the Grass Roots, 557

Moore, David G., 405

Moore, H. Frazier, 55

Moore, John L., 416

More Than News, 579

More Than You Want to Know About Public Service Announcements, 105

Morgan, David, 507, 508

Morigi, Karolyn R., 382

Morrison, Catherine, 422

Mulkern, John R., 420

Museum Public Relations, 631

Myers, Mildred S., 450

Nadel, Mark V., 406

Nagelschmidt, Joseph S., 387

Nager, Norman R., 125, 126

Napoles, Veronica, 332

Napolitan, Joseph, 552

National Directory of Corporate Public Affairs, 167
National Directory of Newsletters and Reporting Services, 152
National Directory of Weekly Newspapers, 159
National Investor Relations Institute, 205, 377
National Radio Publicity Directory, 160
National School Public Relations Association, 604
National Society for the Study of Communication, 218
National Trade and Professional Associations of the United States, 178
Nature of Public Relations, The, 54
Nelson, Richard A., 350
Nelson, Roberta, 633
Nessen, Ron, 529
New Corporate Philanthropy, The, 429
New Directions for Institutional Advancement, 609
New Kingmakers, The, 545
New Perspectives on Political Advertising, 471
New Politics, The, 34
New Style in Election Campaigns, The, 541
New Technology and Public Relations, 108
Newman, Bruce I., 276
News Bureaus in the United States, 165
News Connection, The, 100
News for Investors, 258
News from the White House, 522
Newsgathering in Washington, 33
Newsletters Directory, 152
Newsom, Doug, 56, 57
Newspaperman's President, The, 539
Newswork (series), 499, 500, 501
Newton, Charles G., Jr., 356
NICEM Indexes (series), 298
  online version, 304
Nichols, Donald R., 375
Nimchuk, John, 152
Nimmo, Dan D., 33, 58, 471, 472, 473, 475, 553, 554
1972 Presidential Campaign, The, 542

Ninety Seconds to Tell It All, 395
No Comment: An Executive's Essential Guide to the News Media, 392
Nolte, Lawrence W., 59, 127
Nonprofit Organization Handbook, 584
Norris, James S., 60
Norton, Alice, 277
Nowlan, Stephen E., 128

O'Brien, Richard, 465
O'Donnell, Victoria, 11
O'Dwyer's Directory of Corporate Communications, 168
O'Dwyer's Directory of Public Relations Executives, 169
O'Dwyer's Directory of Public Relations Firms, 170
O'Dwyer's PR Services Report, 207
Olasky, Marvin N., 74
Olins, Wally, 333, 334
On Deadline, 114
Only by Public Consent, 25
Opinion Makers, The, 510
Opinion of the Publics, 14
Opportunities in Public Relations, 192
Organization and Staffing of Corporate Public Affairs, 384
Organizational Communication, 272
Orman, John M., 530
Ornstein, Norman J., 590
Other Government, The, 511
Other Side of the Story, The, 80
Overcoming Opposition, 353

PAC Directory, The, 175
PAC Handbook, The, 419
PAC Power, 423
Packaging the Presidency, 549
PACs Americana, 176
PACs and Parties, 418
P.A.I.S. International, 314. *See also Public Affairs Information Service Bulletin (P.A.I.S.)*
Paisley, William J., 591
Paletz, David L., 397, 509

Parkhurst, William, 129
Patterson, Thomas E., 568, 569
Pavlik, John V., 15
Pearson, Roberta E., 397
Pentagon Propaganda Machine, The, 492
People Machine, The, 30
Perica, Esther, 628
Permanent Campaign, The, 544
Permit, Steven E., 483
Perry, James M., 34
Perspectives in Public Relations, 42
Persuasion Explosion, The, 19
Persuasion: Understanding, Practice and Analysis, 66
Persuasive Public Relations for Libraries, 628
Phantom Politics, 550
Philanthropy and the Business Corporation, 427
Pickens, Judy E., 130
Pimlott, John A. R., 35
Pinsdorf, Marion K., 357
Planning, Implementing and Evaluating Targeted Communication Programs, 137
Police-Community Relations, 281
Political Campaign Debates, 565
Political Communication and Persuasion, 232
Political Communication and Public Opinion in America, 58
Political Communication Bulletin, 233
Political Communication: Issues and Strategies for Research, 470
Political Communication Yearbook, 471, 475
Political Handbook for Health Professionals, A, 616
Political Image Merchants, The, 548
Political Marketing: An Approach to Campaign Strategy, 551
Political Marketing: Readings and an Annotated Bibliography, 276
Political Persuaders, The, 553
Political Power and the Press, 513
Politics and Television Re-viewed, 563
Politics and the Corporate Chief Executive, 405

Politics in Public Service Advertising on Television, 397
Politics of Lying, The, 515
Pollard, James E., 36
Porter, William E., 62, 531
Portraying the President, 520
Powell, Jody, 80
Power of Public Relations, The, 2
Powers That Be, The, 496
PR as in President, 547
PR: How the Public Relations Industry Writes the News, 5
PR News, 208
PR Newswire, 316
PR Reporter, 209
Practical Guide to Consumer Service Management and Operations, 360
Practical Handbook of Public Relations, 187
Practical PR for School Library Media Centers, 625
Practical Public Relations, 95
Practice of Public Relations, The, 63, 115
Precision Public Relations, 113
Premises for Propaganda, 69
Preparing Effective Presentations, 122
President and the Public, The, 519
President Nixon and the Press, 523
Presidential Communication, 517
Presidential Election Show, The, 560
Presidential Leadership in Advancement Activities, 609
Presidential Leadership of Public Opinion, 24
Presidential Secrecy and Deception, 530
Presidential Studies Quarterly, 234
Presidential Television, 567
Presidents and the Press, The, 36
Presidents and the Press: The Nixon Legacy, 533
Press and the State, The, 488
Press in Washington, The, 27
Press, Party and Presidency, 580
Print Media Editorial Calendars, 161
PRLink, 315
Processing the News, 578
Professional Development Guide, 188

Professional's Guide to Public Relations Services, 283
Professional's Guide to Publicity, 141
Promoting Your Cause, 96
Propaganda and Communication in World History, 72
Propaganda and Persuasion, 11
Propaganda in an Open Society, 75
Proxy Issues Report, 259
PsycINFO, 317
  CD-ROM version, 317
Public Affairs Council, 196
Public Affairs Handbook, 387
Public Affairs in Financial Services, 466
Public Affairs Information Service Bulletin (P.A.I.S.), 299
  online version, 314
Public Affairs Review, 196
Public Communication Campaigns, 591
Public Encounter, The, 494
Public Hearings, Procedures and Strategies, 482
Public Image of Big Business in America, 1880-1940, The, 70
Public Interest Profiles, 179
Public Management Institute, 131, 180
Public Media Center, 586
Public Opinion, 29, 256
Public Opinion Quarterly, 235
Public Persuader, The, 490
Public Relations
  Bernays, 92
  Jefkins, 52
  Norris, 60
  United Kingdom, 197
Public Relations: A Comprehensive Bibliography, 267
Public Relations: A Contemporary Approach, 49
Public Relations: A Scientific Approach, 135
Public Relations and American Democracy, 35
Public Relations and Business, 1900-1929, 37
Public Relations and Communications for Natural Resource Managers, 479
Public Relations and Community, 381

Public Relations and Presidential Campaigns, 543
Public Relations and the Law, 41
Public Relations and Survey Research, 38
Public Relations as Communication Management, 47
Public Relations Body of Knowledge, 184
Public Relations Bibliography, 282
Public Relations Can Be Fun and Easy, 617
Public Relations Career Directory, 191
Public Relations Cases, 112
Public Relations: Concepts and Practices, 64
Public Relations for Libraries, 623
Public Relations for Nursing Homes, 615
Public Relations for Public Libraries, 627
Public Relations for Schools, 610
Public Relations for the Entrepreneur and the Growing Business, 138
Public Relations Guide for CPAs, 464
Public Relations Handbook, 85
Public Relations in Action, 61
Public Relations in an Era of Public Involvement, 467
Public Relations in Local Government, 480
Public Relations in the Marketing Mix, 110
Public Relations in the 1980s, 4
Public Relations: Information Sources, 277
Public Relations Is Your Business, 102
Public Relations Job Finder, The, 190
Public Relations Journal, 171, 198
Public Relations Law, 41
Public Relations Management: A Casebook, 65
Public Relations Management by Objectives, 125
Public Relations Practices: Managerial Case Studies and Problems, 46
Public Relations: Principles, Cases and Problems, 55
Public Relations Programming and Production, 98

Public Relations, Promotions and Fund-Raising for Athletic and Physical Education Programs, 601
Public Relations/Publicity, 109
Public Relations Quarterly, 199
Public Relations Review, 113, 200, 282, p. 42
Public Relations Society of America, 171, 181, 182, 188, 191, 198, 278, 315
Public Relations Strategies and Tactics, 68
Public Relations, the Edward L. Bernayses and the American Scene, 274
Public Relations: The Profession and the Practice, 45
Public Relations: What Research Tells Us, 15
Public Relations World Congress, 4
Public Relations Writer in a Computer Age, 67
Public Relations Writing: Form and Style, 56
Publicity Handbook, The, 143
Publicity: How to Get It, 465
Publicity: How to Make the Media Work for You, 117
Publishing Newsletters, 116

Quill, 245

Race for the Presidency, 559
Ragan Report, 210
Raising the Bottom Line, 445
Ranney, Austin, 570
Rasberry, Robert W., 474
Rating America's Corporate Conscience, 441
Raucher, Alan R., 37
Redefining Corporate-Federal Relations, 404
Reilly, Robert T., 61
Register, 171
Rein, Irving J., 16
Religious Public Relations Council, 598
Religious Public Relations Handbook, 598

Reporters and Officials, 512
Research in Corporate Social Performance and Policy, 228
Resources in Education, 290
Reuss, Carol, 369
Rice, Betty, 627
Rice, Ronald E., 591
Rich, Stuart U., 467
Ricks, David R., 462
Ridgway, Judith, 132
Riggs, Lew, 621
Rise of Political Consultants, The, 555
Risley, Curtis, 133
Rivers, William L., 510, 511
Roalman, Arthur R., 376, 377
Robinson, Edward J., 38
Roeder, Edward, 176
Rogers, Henry C., 81, 134
Rogers' Rules for Success, 134
Ross, Irwin, 39
Ross, J. David, 609
Ross, Robert D., 388
Rostow, Jerome M., 443
Roth, Robert F., 463
Rotman, Morris, 192
Rowland, A. Westley, 608, 609
Rowland, Howard R., 609
Rubin, Richard L., 580
Ruffner, Robert H., 592
Rummel, Kathleen K., 628
Rumor in the Marketplace, 329
Ryan, Mike H., 407
Ryans, Cynthia C., 279

Sabato, Larry J., 423, 555
Sahai, Baldeo, 135
Saldich, Anne R., 571
Sales and Marketing Management, 257
Salinger, Pierre, 40
Sanders, Keith R., 471, 473, 475
Savage, Robert, 554
Say It Safely, 90
Schiller, Herbert I., 17
Schmertz, Herbert, 338
Schneider, William, 13
Scholars, Dollars, and Public Policy, 430

School and Community Relations, The, 605

Schorr, Daniel, 82

Schram, Martin, 572

Schramm, Wilbur, 62

Schuettinger, Robert L., 430

Scott, Alan, 57

SEC, the Securities Markets, and Financial Communications, The, 372

Seitel, Fraser, P., 63

Selame, Elinor, 136, p. 58

Selame, Joe, 136, p. 58

Selling of the President, 1968, The, 31

Selnow, Gary W., 137

Sethi, S. Prakash, 339, 340, 444

Setting Up a European Public Relations Operation, 456

Seymour, Ure, Colin, 532

Shanklin, William L., 279

Shapiro, Irving S., 408

Sharpe, Melvin L., 95

Shayon, Diana R., 128

Shearer, Benjamin F., 280

Sheldon, Bernice E., 588

Sheth, Jagdish N., 276

Shipper, Frank, 409

Sigal, Leon V., 512

Silk, Leonard, 342

Silvis, Donn E., 369

Simon, Morton J., 41

Simon, Raymond, 42, 64, 65

Simons, Herbert W., 66

Small, William J., 513

Small College Advancement Program, The, 613

Social Audit for Management, The, 447

Social Auditing, 450

Social Change and Corporate Strategy, 379

Social Issues Service, 258, 259

Social Science Monitor for Public Relations and Advertising Executives, 211

Social Sciences Citation Index, 300
online version, 319

Social Sciences Index, 301
online version, 318

Social Scisearch, 319
print version, 300

Social Strategy and Corporate Structure, 439

Sociological Abstracts, 320

Soderberg, Norman R., 138

Sorauf, Frank J., 424

Spear, Joseph C., 533

Speier, Hans, 72

Sperber, Nathaniel N., 139

Spero, Robert, 573

Spitzer, Carlton E., 445, 502

Sponsored Film, The, 118

Spot, The, 561

Spragens, William C., 534

Standard Rate and Data Service, Inc., 161

Stanley, Guy D., 358

Starck, Kenneth, 381

State Department, Press and Pressure Groups, The, 489

Status and Trends of Public Relations Education in United States Senior Colleges and Universities, 185

Steckmest, Francis W., 389

Steele, Fritz, 370

Steele, Richard W., 75

Steinberg, Charles S., 18, 514

Steiner, George A., 451

Stevens, Art, 19

Stoller, Martin R., 16

Straight Stuff, 516

Strategic Issues Management, 349

Strategic Marketing for Educational Institutions, 607

Strategic Planning Marketing and Public Relations, and Fund-Raising in Higher Education, 279

Strategic Public Relations Counseling, 126

Strategies for Access to Public Service Advertising, 586

Stridsberg, Albert B., 341

Studies of the Modern Corporation, 323

Studying and Addressing Community Needs, 390

Subliminal Politics, 472

Successful Governmental Relations, 609

Successful Media Relations, 132

Successful Public Relations for Colleges and Universities, 606

Successful Public Relations Techniques, 131

Sullivan, Frank C., 468

Sumrall, Velma, 599

Supreme Court and Its Publics, The, 485

Surveying Institutional Constituencies, 609

Swanson, Carl L., 407

Syndicated Columnists, 162

Tarver, Jerry, 140

Task Force on Corporate Social Performance, 452

Taxonomy of Concepts in Communication, A, 84

Technique of Political Lying, The, 474

Tedlow, Richard S., 76

Telepolitics, 574

Television and Presidential Politics, 562

Television and the Presidential Elections, 564

Television and the Red Menace, 505

Television Contacts, 164

Tell It to the World, 111

Telling the Story of the Local Church, 599

Terwoord, Carole, 534

This Business of Issues, 345

This Is PR, 57

Thompson, Kenneth W., 535, 536

Thornton, Barbara C., 619

Three Press Secretaries on the Presidency and the Press, 535

Trade and Industry Index, 321

Troy, Kathryn, 390, 432, 433, 466

Truitt, Richard H., 126

Trustee's Role in Advancement, 609

Turner, Kathleen J., 537

TV News, 163

TV PR, 99

Twentieth Century Fund Task Force on the Military and the Media, 487

23 Most Common Mistakes in Public Relations, The, 91

Ulloth, Dana R., 488

Ultimate Insiders, The, 500

Understanding Academic Law, 609

Understanding and Increasing Foundation Support, 609

Underwood, Bob, 629

United States Political Science Documents, 302

Unruh, Adolph, 610

Unseeing Eye, The, 569

Unstable Ground, The, 444

U.S. Business Support for International Public Service Activities, 453

Using Charts and Graphs, 142

Using New Communications Technologies, 124

Using the Mass Media, 609

Vance Bibliographies, 281

Vermeer, Jan P., 556

Vested Interest, 79

Vibbert, Steven L., 47, 86

Video Monitor, 212

Views from the Top, 443

Visible Library, The, 629

Vogel, David, 436, 446

Voice of Government, The, 502

Wadsworth, Anne J., 273

Walker, Albert, 184, 185, 282

Walking the Tightrope, 81

Walling, Donovan R., 611

Walsh, Frank E., 41, 46, 67

War That Hitler Won, The, 71

Warner, Rawleigh, Jr., 342

Washington Journalism Review, 246

Washington Lobby, The, 416

Washington Lobbyists, The, 32

Washington Reporters, The, 501

Washington Representatives, 177

Webb, Stanley G., 469

Weidenbaum, Murray L., 410, 411

Weinberger, Marvin I., 175

Weiner, Richard, 141, 165, 283

Weingand, Darlene E., 630

Welch, Patrice A., 609

West, Philip T., 612
West Glen Films, 292
Western Political Quarterly, 236
What Price PACs?, 424
What Washington Said, 504
When Consumers Complain, 359
When Government Speaks, 476
When It Hits the Fan, 355
White, Graham J., 538
White, Jan V., 142
White House Press on the Presidency, The, 536
Who's Who in Public Relations, 172
Wilcox, Dennis L., 68, 127
Wilhelmsen, Frederick D., 574
Williams, Dorothy F., 609
Williams, Herbert L., 539
Willier, Robert A., 610
Willis, Don L., 397
Willmer, Wesley K., 609, 613
Wise, David, 515
With Kennedy, 40

Without Bias: A Guidebook for Non-discriminatory Communication, 130
Wolff Olins Guide to Corporate Identity, The, 334
Wood, Robert J., 83
Working Press of the Nation, The, 166
Writing for Public Relations, 107
Writing in Public Relations Practice, 56
Wyckham, Robert G., 284
Wyckoff, Gene, 43

Yale, David R., 143
Yarrington, Roger, 593
Your Future in a Public Relations Career, 186
Yudof, Mark G., 476

Zisk, Betty H., 557

Subject Index

Unless otherwise indicated, reference is to entry number.

Accountants, 448, 464
Accrediting Council on Education in Journalism and Mass Communication, pp. 29, 33
Advertising, 90, 226, 249, 327
 advocacy, 338-342
 political, 471, 490, 549, 561, 573
 public service, 105, 397, 586
Agricultural Relations Council, p. 25
Air traffic controllers' strike, 508
American Association for Public Opinion Research, p. 29
American Association of Fund-Raising Counsel, p. 25
American Association of Political Consultants, 555, p. 25
American Bankers Association, p. 30
American Business Conference, p. 30
American Chemical Society, p. 30
American Council of Life Insurance, p. 30
American Dairy Association and Dairy Council, p. 31
American Institute for Political Communication, p. 82
American Management Association, 322
American Medical Association, p. 31
American Petroleum Institute, p. 31
American Pharmaceutical Association, p. 31
American Political Science Association, p. 29
American Society for Hospital Marketing and Public Relations, p. 25
American Society of Association Executives, p. 26
Armed forces. See United States, Defense Department
Arts and Business Council, p. 31
Association for Business Communication, p. 26

Association for Education in Journalism and Mass Communication, pp. 30, 32
Attitude change, 12. See also Political attitudes

Ball State University, p. 34
Bank Marketing Association, p. 26
Bernays, Edward L., 274, pp. xi, xii, xiii, 11, 12
Boston University, p. 34
Bowling Green State University, p. 34
Brown, Jerry, 550
Burson-Marsteller Information Services, p. 12
Business Committee for the Arts, p. 32
Business Roundtable, p. 31

California State University, Fullerton, p. 34
Career planning, 186, 188, 190. See also Job descriptions
Carter, Jimmy, 80, 520
CASE Reference Center, p. 12
Celebrities, 16, 465
Center for Corporate Public Involvement, p. 32
Chamber of Commerce of the United States, p. 31
Chemical Manufacturers Association, p. 31
Churches, 598, 599
Colleges and universities. See Higher education
Communication research, 1, 11, 12, 15, 38, 62, 84, 86, 211, 213-221, 271, 272, 289, 297
Community relations, 378, 381, 390, 440
Conference Board, 324, p. 74

Consumers, 359, 446. *See also* Corporations, consumer relations
Corporations, 222, 224, 225, 311
  consumer relations, 360-363
  educational activities, 335-337, 364
  financial reporting, 252, 372. *See also*
    Investor relations
  image, 136, 330, 332, 333, 334. *See also*
    Graphic design
  media relations, 114, 391, 393, 394, 395
  philanthropy, 425-433
  political activities, 23, 44, 73, 398-409.
    See also Lobbying; Political
    action committees
  public affairs activities, 196, 380, 384,
    385, 386, 437. *See also* Community relations; Crisis management; Issues management
  public relations, 2, 9, 25, 37, 73, 74,
    76, 128, 193, 327-469
  social responsibility, 223, 228, 434-441,
    444, 445
Council for Advancement and Support
  of Education, pp. 12, 26
Council on Economic Priorities, p. 32
Crisis management, 93, 343, 348, 352,
  354-357

Dissertations, 291, 294, 295, 309

Educational media, 292, 298, 304, 337
Eisenhower, Dwight D., 521, 532
Eleutherian Mills Historical Library, p. 12
Employee manuals, 89
Employee relations, 266, 365-370
Ethics, 25, 57
European Confederation of Public
  Relations, p. 26

Falklands War, 497, 503
Filmmaking, 118
Financial intermediaries, 466
Ford, Gerald, 520, 529
Forestry, 467
Foundation for Economic Education, p. 32

Foundation for Public Relations Research
  and Education. *See* Institute for
  Public Relations Research and
  Education
Fund raising, 264, 265, 269, 270, 582,
  594, 595, 602

General Motors Corporation, p. 12
Government and the press, 484, 486-489,
  493, 499, 502, 509, 510, 512-514.
  See also Presidents; Press conferences; names of government
  departments
Government information. *See* Government publicity
Government publicity, 27, 33, 35, 476,
  481, 483, 490, 502, 507, 508, 515.
  See also Government and the
  press; Propaganda
Graphic design, 136, 142, 330, 331
Great Britain, public relations, 52, 102,
  115, 132

Handicapped, 633
Health services, 616, 619, 621. *See also*
  Hospitals; Nursing homes
Higher education, 263, 600, 602, 606-609,
  612, 613
Hill, John W., p. 11
Hitler, Adolph, 71
Hospitals, 614, 618, 620

India, public relations, 135
Industrial publicity, 104
Industry and government, 406, 410, 411.
  See also Corporations, political
  activities
Influence, 7, 11, 12, 17, 66, 398. *See also*
  Attitude change
Institute for Public Relations Research and
  Education, pp. 30, 33, 45-46
Institute of Public Relations, p. 26
Insurance, 442, 466
Insurance Information Institute, p. 31

International Association of Business Communicators, p. 26

International Communication Association, p. 27

International public relations, 4, 111, 194, 426, 431, 453-461

International Public Relations Association, pp. 27, 32-33, 78

Investor relations, 204, 205, 254, 258, 259, 371, 374-377, 446

Investor Responsibility Research Center, 325

Iran hostage crisis, 503

Issue Management Association, p. 27

Issues management, 202, 338, 344-347, 349-351, 353, 358

Job descriptions, 6, 191

Johnson, Lyndon B., 537

Journalism, 5, 90, 218-221, 242, 245, 246, 295, 296, 297, 575, 577. *See also* Government and the press; News; Reporters and reporting

Journalism and Mass Communications Library, University of Illinois, p. 12

Journalism Library, University of Missouri, p. 12

Kennedy, John F., 40, 484, 524

Kent State University, p. 34

Lee, Ivy, 26, 74, p. 11

Legal issues, 41, 90, 130, 476

Libraries, 623, 626, 628, 630
   public, 624, 627, 629
   school, 625

Library Public Relations Council, p. 27

Lobbying, 23, 32, 79, 281, 412-416, 581. *See also* Corporations, political activities

Local government, 477, 480

Marketing, 8, 16, 110, 227, 250, 255, 257, 284, 462, 463, 551, 607, 620, 630

Mass Communications History Center, p. 11

Mass media, 62, 88, 203, 214, 216, 240, 280, 491, 496, 506, 509, 576, 579, 580. *See also* News; Radio; Television

Media Institute, The, p. 32

Milton Caniff Library, p. 12

Museums, 631

National Association of Broadcasters, p. 32

National Association of Government Communicators, p. 27

National Association of Home Builders, p. 31

National Association of Manufacturers, pp. 11, 31

National Council for Community Relations, p. 27

National Investor Relations Institute, p. 27

National Rifle Association of America, p. 31

National School Public Relations Association, p. 27

National Society of Fund Raising Executives, p. 28

Natural resources management, 479

News, 5, 244, 373, 496, 506, 512, 513, 524, 527, 528, 572, 575, 577, 578

Newsletters, 116, 158

Nieman-Grant Reading Room, University of Wisconsin, p. 12

Nixon, Richard M., 31, 43, 484, 523, 526-528, 531-533, 542, 567

Nonprofit organizations, 260-262, 584, 586, 588, 589, 592, 597. *See also* Churches; Health services; Hospitals, Libraries, Museums; Nursing homes; Schools; Social services

Northwestern University, p. 34

Nursing homes, 615, 617

Ohio State University, p. 34

Ohio University, p. 34

Oklahoma State University, p. 34

Organization theory, 1

Page, Arthur W., p. 11
Parks management. *See* Recreation
    management
Performing arts, 596
Persuasion. *See* Influence
Physical education programs, 601
Police, 281
Political action committees, 173, 175, 176,
    399, 407, 409, 416-424
Political attitudes, 472, 578
Political campaigns, 30, 31, 34, 43, 273,
    276, 402, 403, 540-560, 562, 564,
    565, 567, 568, 570, 572, 575
Political communication, 58, 232-234, 302,
    470, 473, 475, 491, 504, 578, 580
Political consultants, 28, 34, 58, 543-545,
    548, 552, 553, 555
Political science, 229-231, 236, 291, 302
Presidents, 24, 36, 234, 275, 516, 517,
    519, 520, 522, 525, 530, 532,
    534-536. *See also* names of
    individual presidents
Press conferences, 24, 36, 40, 122, 536
Pressure groups, 123, 557, 581, 590, 591
Professional corporations, 469
Professional standards, 171, p. xiii
Professionalism, 4, 9
Propaganda, 11, 69, 71, 72, 75, 474
Psychology, 317. *See also* Social
    psychology
Public Affairs Council, p. 71
Public meetings, 482
Public opinion, 13, 17, 29, 235, 256, 578,
    579. *See also* Political attitudes
Public opinion polls, 13, 34, 558
Public relations
    education, 181, 182, 183, 185, 290,
        310, p. 34
    history, 20, 26, 37, 42, 70, 74, 76
    management, 65, 97, 125
    news, 198, 206-210, 315
    research, 15, 200, p. 38
Public Relations Society of America,
    pp. xii, 12, 25, 28, 30, 32-33, 46
Public Relations Student Society of
    America, p. 30
Public Relations World Congress, p. 78
Public speaking, 106, 140

Public utilities, 468
Public Utilities Communicators Associa-
    tion, p. 28
Publicity, 5, 16, 39, 78, 109, 117, 127,
    129, 141, 143, 465, 585. *See also*
    Government publicity; Industrial
    publicity; Television publicity

Radio, 105, 119
Railroad Public Relations Association,
    p. 28
Recreation management, 478
Religious Public Relations Council, p. 28
Reporters and reporting, 5, 27, 33, 373,
    396, 501, 507, 508, 511, 512,
    546. *See also* Government and
    the press; Journalism; Press
    conferences
Roosevelt, Franklin D., 75, 518, 538
Rumor, 329

San Jose State University, p. 34
Schools, 195, 310, 603-605, 610, 611. *See
    also* Higher education; Physical
    education programs
Seely G. Mudd Manuscript Library, p. 11
Small business, 138
Social accounting, 447-452
Social psychology, 7, 238, 239
Social services, 593, 632, 633. *See also*
    Health services
Society of Consumer Affairs Professionals
    in Business, p. 28
Sociology, 237, 320
Sonnenberg, Benjamin, 77
Southern Mississippi State, p. 34
State Governmental Affairs Council, p. 29
Syracuse University, p. 34

Technical Association of the Pulp and
    Paper Industry, p. 31
Technological innovations, 108, 124
Television, 212, 241
    news, 82, 505, 563, 572
    political uses of, 30, 34, 43, 560-574
    publicity, 99, 105, 119, 335

Tobacco Institute, p. 31
Truman, Harry S., 539

Unions, 79, 622
United States
  Congress, 486, 500
  culture, 22
  Defense Department, 487, 492, 495, 498
  President. *See* Presidents
  State Department, 489
  Supreme Court, 485
United States Army Information Center,
    p. 12
University of Alabama, p. 34
University of Florida, p. 34
University of Georgia, p. 34
University of Maryland, p. 34
University of Northern Illinois, p. 34
University of Oklahoma, p. 34

University of Oregon, p. 34
University of South Florida, p. 34
University of Southern California, p. 34
University of Tennessee, p. 34
University of Texas, p. 34
University of Utah, p. 34
University of Wisconsin-Madison, p. 34

Vietnam War, 504, 505, 537
Volunteer service, 587

Watergate, 82, 474, 527
Women Executives in Public Relations,
    p. 29
Women in Communications, p. 29
Women in Government Relations, p. 29
Writing, 56, 67, 94, 107, 133